D1482410

The Success Trail:

Learn to Win with a Marathon Runner's Mindset

Jack Perconte

Ordering Information: Quantity sales. Special discounts are available on quantity purchases by corporations, associations, and others. For details, contact the "Special Sales Department" at the address above. The Success Trail/Jack Perconte—1st edition

LCCN 2021907740

ISBN. 978-0-9981709-4-7

1. Marathon Training

2. Running and Jogging

3. Sports Psychology

The Success Trail:

Learn to Win with a Marathon Runner's Mindset

My story is a marathon-length "Pep Talk" dedicated to runners, athletes, and anyone interested in learning the mindset to compete and live up to their potential. Unfortunately, no magic solution exists to winning — it takes a step-by-step journey!

Contents

1
The Forward Mindset

A Dream

The crowd is on their feet. A grizzled old athlete who knows his better days are behind him is defying Father Time. He is galloping like the wind and about to win. Incredulous may be the best way to describe the scene. The athlete's weathered face portrays the same, along with another look – confusion. He expects to approach a catcher, umpire, home plate, and people on their feet clapping in a vast stadium. Instead, he sees a tape as he runs through a gauntlet of people cheering madly.

I wake in a sweat and wonder what it means? The explanation is simple. My sporting life has been baseball and running. I have happy sleep visions of scoring the winning run and finishing marathons. And nightmares of misplaying a ground ball and tripping when out for a jog. The dream is a model of life itself — one moment is fantastic, the next one, not so much.

"If You want something you've never had, you must be willing to do something you've never done."

Thomas Jefferson

In this prescient quote, Thomas Jefferson details the slippery path to accomplishment.

Develop Fundamental Beliefs

Do you ever wonder what it takes to do something noteworthy? I know a little about it from reaching two cherished athletic goals, the Major Leagues and 14 marathons. Thomas Jefferson is right on, and I would like to add to his proclamation, "Nothing meaningful comes from short and easy." Finishing a marathon and making dreams come true takes a long and hard road. The benefits of long and hard are discovering yourself and your competitive makeup. When you strive to go high and far, life is purposeful, which is the way it should be.

My running story begins with a few fundamental beliefs.

The Boss, Bruce Springsteen sang,

"Cause tramps like us

Baby, we were born to run."

And Christopher McDougall wrote in his book *Born to Run,*

"If you don't think you weren't born to run, you're not only denying history. You're denying who you are."

I'll accept being those because I know I was born to run. To all the tramps and deniers out there, it's time to get moving.

Christopher also writes,

"You don't stop running because you get old; you get old because you stop running."

That's my belief, too, to keep moving and stick to it forever. I hope, anyway, knowing experience is my friend, but age isn't.

Follow Those Who Have Gone Before

I am not an expert or world-class marathoner by any means, so I cannot give you the top runners' perspective. I can't even imagine how it is possible to run that far under two and a half hours. Nor can I fathom the amount of training one would have to run those times. As for me, I consider running under five hours for the 26.2 miles a miraculous feat.

However, now in training for my 15th marathon, I have the background to write about traveling far on foot, regardless of not trying to break records. My experience allows me to tell you what it is like for amateur runners who love running and pushing themselves beyond where they thought they could go. This guide will help those interested in knowing how to commit and be their best at their goals.

I must warn you, though. Sometimes, it may sound like I am discouraging running a marathon — that is not my intent. But the frequently-mentioned anguish can make it seem that way. The fact is finishing a marathon is daunting, and the training is even more robust. My goal is to help "the trier" feel as I do when taking on an arduous task — alive, goal-oriented, and disciplined.

Additionally, I was not a great baseball player, but I did what it took to make the top level. That quest gave valuable insight into the training and dedication needed to be a proven athlete. It is where I figured out what it takes to compete and persevere. Most importantly, I know my past had shown me how to finish when the odds seemed against me. So, I will not say, "If I can run a marathon, anybody can." I know playing Major League Baseball is a significant advantage for running a marathon. What I can say is the two struggles give me a perspective few others have. I often tell my baseball players that one learns more from failure than from success. I believe that, so I know I have a ton to say with my many setbacks in baseball and marathon running.

Find the Route

Perhaps like me, you have heard the expression, "Running is a metaphor for life." I agree. One day and one mile, one has clarity, the next time and mile, everything comes crashing down. Life and running are not smooth-flowing excursions. Both involve many moments when joy and the finish line seem far away.

Many things go into high performance. Talent helps with the substantial, necessary physical toll athletes require, but it only takes one so far. Other factors, like experience, resilience, and perseverance, play a huge role. It's mostly the cerebral aspect that separates the advancers from those who falter. Developing the right mindset separates the achievers from the wannabes.

Create A Purposeful Attitude

Running and training for a marathon is hard work, no question, but spectacular spells come too. Sometimes, my feet barely touch the ground. Those may be fleeting moments, but the elusive life focus and peace of mind arrive, and all is well in the world. The most exciting thing is running has helped me clarify the items that go into a successful life voyage.

I've come to realize the importance of:

1. Never getting far from doing the things you love. At the young age of 67, I coach baseball and keep scampering along the running trails. Both activities give me purpose and youthful sensations. When you find something that inspires, grab hold, and never let it go. Then, use what you learn for others and other life endeavors. The marathon may be long, but life is short.

2. Never stop searching for and attempting new ambitions and bucket list items because they bring meaning to life. Many undertakings are not straightforward but going through life and never giving them a try creates avoidable regrets. It's critical not to put yearnings off for long because some may take a lifetime to reach.

3. Learning to apply an uncommon daring, a tank full of guts, and above-average stamina to reach higher than before. Without those, one's full potential will be elusive.

Goals are attainable for those who put their heart and soul and, in athletics, body into it.

4. Turning "challenge" into "the necessary" to accomplish the most trying endeavors. If you get to the point of doing something because "you must," it becomes you. When you rely on an activity as part of a perfect day, accomplishing it becomes easier.

5. Giving your all to discover things about yourself you will not find elsewhere.

Believe in the Possible Rewards

Not everyone can run a marathon. Loping long stretches in a single bound requires unique physicality. But everyone can discover what it takes to become a successful runner, athlete, winner, and hero. Being a runner gives you an identity to be proud of and helps with a healthy lifestyle. Learning what it takes to be an athlete helps one flourish in many life areas. A winner is a mindset. It lets you know you have what it takes to succeed, and the pride it brings influences one daily. And who wouldn't want to feel like a hero – a person admired for their dedication and perseverance. Whether others accept you as one or not, to think of yourself in that way is life-altering. I believe it's a worthy accolade when you think of the road it takes to do the doubtful and knowing it's beyond what most people can do.

The incentive and reward are the same — you will be one of the select people in this world who pull the marathon feat off. Less than 1% of people on this planet have finished a marathon. Better yet, it may end up the most outstanding accomplishment of your life. With any struggle, to say, "I gave it everything I had," and "I pushed myself to the limit" is momentous itself. Any of those results are worthy accomplishments no one can ever take away from you. The attempt alone makes it worth it for two reasons — you tried and did your best.

Step Up to Move Forward

I'm frequently asked, "How did you make it to the big leagues?" My initial response is, "That's a great question. I'm not sure what all went into it, except I know it took a lot of work." That response is the same as for another query I now receive, "How have you run so many marathons?" I felt it was time to unearth the solutions to both inquiries. My high-achievement mission details 26.2 intricate steps. Of course, that number is no coincidence when thinking about a marathon. It's a considerable number, no doubt, but a reason exists some people reach their end, and others do not. One doesn't get to the stars without building a solid rocket – A to Z plus two!

Although I will show you how to get as much out of yourself as possible with running, as I have had to do, I believe the success trail is the same and critical for coping with all life challenges. Many solutions are here for those seeking their athletic, working, parenting, or creative potential. Mostly, I hope my tale of success and failure helps you believe you can do anything you set out to do, or at the least, spur you to give your ambitions a try.

I invite you to come along. It will be fun, at least the reading, if not the sweat.

A Marathon Legend Capsule

Grace Personified

One just never knows what life has in store for them.

Imagine you are retiring on Friday, and the day before you hang it up, you discover something about yourself you never knew. Instead of stopping, you become the most successful person in the world in your field. For some people, fate has a way of stepping up in the nick of time.

As hard as it is to admit, I cry easily. Upsetting or inspiring news makes me emotional, and having to tell someone about it often brings more teardrops. It's just me. I cried when reading about this person, especially seeing a way-too-young death after a life well-lived. For a hint to that person, I pose this question that I realize only hard-core running fans will know. Who was the first non-American inducted into the United States National Distance Running Hall of Fame?

After a successful running career at lower distances globally, Norwegian Grete Waitz was retiring to her school-teacher profession. Before that, however, she entered the New York Marathon at the last moment, after encouragement from her husband. Because of the late entry, her bib number wasn't in the official program. Grete later stated that they treated New York as a second honeymoon, and the race was another thing to do while in New York. She knew little about marathons and had never run more than 13 miles at a time in her life. So, the

26.2 miles would be nearly impossible. According to the New York times, "She said the last 10 miles of the race were agony, and she was so angry at her husband that when she crossed the finish line, she tore off her shoes and flung them at him." "I'll never do this stupid thing again," she yelled.

All distance runners can relate to that feeling, and it's kind of cool to note a high-caliber athlete had the sensation of us average runners. Wait a minute! What? Never mind. It turns out Grete won the New York marathon that day, and by the way, set a women's world record in doing so. That, of course, is "greatness" because the "average" never experiences the impossible.

The experience hooked her on the Marathon, and she trained, set more records for years to come, and inspired people worldwide. Getting hooked is how it works for many of us; it doesn't matter how unbearable it gets, running slips into one's soul. She won the New York Marathon nine times and set the world record many times. She won too many events to mention here.

Impressive stuff, sure, but what brought the tears were the words spoken about her. For example:

"Humility and athleticism made her a singularly graceful champion" – New York Times.

"What will endure forever is that she was able to balance a competitive career with the most gracious lifestyle, and a character that emanated goodwill" – Joan Benoit Samuelson

"Every sport should have a true champion like Grete, a woman with such dignity and humanity and modesty." – George Hirsch, the chairman of the New York Road Runners.

"She is our sport's towering legend." – Mary Wittenberg, New York Road Runners President.

It's one thing to be a tremendous athlete, but as everyone knows, that adjective doesn't always or often extend beyond the playing fields. When I hear the words - humility, gracious, goodwill, dignity, humanity, modesty, and legend - I take note, cry, and hope people like her are in our kids' history books. Athletes, especially youth ones, need role models, and Grete fits the bill like few others. Another thing difficult for me to admit is Grete finished the New York marathon in less than half the time it took me to do it. Oh well, I can live with that just knowing I traveled the ground she made hallowed.

My Story: A Disappointing Win

Each mile I travel only means

The more I have to go

What's wrong with wanting more?

If you can fly - then soar!

With all there is - why settle for

Just a piece of sky?

Barbara Streisand *"A Piece of Sky"*

Tailored to Win

My goal for each marathon has been to finish the race and live to talk about it. I know that sounds a little overdramatic, but it fits the purpose when answering the frequent inquiry of "What time do you expect to finish?" Of course, stretches came during the fourteen marathons that such a dire eventuality crossed my mind. The fantastic news is I finished each one, and the feat gives me the same pride I gained from being on the major league stage.

But even though satisfied with the outcomes, sometimes in sports, a win feels more like a loss. For example, from mile 17 on in my New York marathon, it was an enormous gut-check. That is not unusual because it comes in all marathons, but it came much earlier than expected this time. Typically, I will not walk any until mile 23, if at all,

11

but there I was, spent already. I did not spill the guts during the race, but after was a different story. I realize it's the price the athlete occasionally pays. Like other times in my sporting life, I just knew I had to find a way after everything in me, except my heart, said stop. Let me go back to the beginning.

I was sure everything was in place to set my personal best time. Even though I read the course was challenging, I thought it was there for the taking. The weather was perfect, and even with 55,000 runners, the first mile was the only time maneuvering was an issue. The starting atmosphere was electric with speakers blaring Old Blue Eyes, Frank Sinatra, "New York, New York." We began over the Verrazano bridge with incredible views of New York to the left and right. I am ecstatic as much as anyone with having 26.2 miles to run can be.

We entered Brooklyn with the streets lined with fans 6 and 7 deep – so cool. The first 13 miles went smoothly, and the city and crowds were fabulous. I could not even hear my headphones music at some points because of the crowd noise. It reminded me of playing in front of major league crowds, and it felt good. I had every reason to keep rocking the race and enjoy it. It just didn't happen.

Trudging On

At mile 15, I felt something was not right because I was putting out more energy than I should at this point. The athlete in me held out hoped I would come around, as sometimes happens, but things did not follow my wish. My spirit couldn't get over the lack of energy for long.

12

It was on to Queens and the most taxing part, over the bridge to Manhattan. It seemed a never-ending stretch that beat me up. It was on to the Bronx and back to Manhattan and Central Park. My weak state did not let me enjoy the picturesqueness. I tried every trick in my "Get in the zone" book to divert the mind from feeling miserable, but none worked for long. Meeting up with family members at mile markers 17 and 19 was some saving grace, but I needed divine intervention, I joke. It's never lucky for the distance runner once the thoughts are only of physical pain and the remaining miles. Once trapped in a dreadful demeanor, each mile seems like six.

If it were training and not the day I had been anticipating for so long, I would have packed it in early. Athletes know some days are not theirs, but my athletic spirit does not allow quitting in a game unless it is the only alternative. As implied, the one bit of optimism comes from knowing I have been in similar troublesome situations. I recall being fourteen years old, and my once rocket arm left me overnight. The big-league dream did not seem promising after becoming stuck with a second baseman's arm at such a young age. In another instance, upon graduating from high school, zero college baseball programs showed interest in me. Once again, the dream seemed a bridge too far. With the odds against me in the race, I refer to the situations which taught me "There is a way, and I must find it" and "I will not let it end before doing everything I can to get what I set out to do."

The competitor in me knows down is not out, and I must keep moving forward. I keep going and try one of many self-pep talks that goes like this – "There will be times one gets to a hill, and a choice is necessary - run-up, walk or stop. The competitor does not choose that third alternative."

I finish! A win, but why do I not feel better about it? The answer lies with the competitor's mindset of believing one should have done better. After the race, I reviewed everything and tried to figure out where things went wrong. What I figured out was, "I don't know," and I refuse to make excuses. It is just another of the reasons they play the games – you just never know. In a glass-half-full way, having to persevere through the physical and mental anguish for 9 miles was an enormous victory. You see, being a winner is about overcoming the heartache of sub-par performances. If I didn't consider myself one, I would have quit. I knew better was possible, and immediately, I knew it would not be my last marathon.

I took these lessons from the race to be better the next time:

Never take anything for granted.

Explore your past to overcome complications.

To quit is not an option.

A setback is only one if you do nothing about it.

Failure does not end dreams.

The New York Marathon was a formidable test, and after was the time to find another mountain to climb. Thankfully, my fighting spirit lived.

2
The Courageous Mindset

A Dream

I am on the 26.2-mile path, but I am shaking with fear after realizing no finish line exists. My mind spins from having no direction. Panic City!

I wake. What's the meaning? A disturbing nightmare whose analysis is simple – confusion and anxiety reign with no destination. Goals are imperative for achievement and avoiding pointless wandering and wasting time.

"Every morning, you have two choices, to sleep with your dreams or to wake up and chase them."

Carmelo Anthony

The answer to Carmelo's options seems obvious, so don't sleep too long.

The success trail needs a solid foundation. Laying pavement will smooth the road to the starting line.

Stairway to success:

1. A Dream

2. Courage

3. Know-how

4. Definition of Winning

Step Up to Your Dreams

I have heard people say, "A million dollars isn't what it used to be." My response is, "Yea, right, but give it to me, and I will find out for myself if true." Others opine, "A marathon is not a big thing anymore." I would say, "Yea, whatever." Deniers may reason it's ordinary because of ultra-marathon runners or the many marathon entrees nowadays. I would respond to the last announcement with, "OK, Hotshot, how many have you run?" Earning a million bucks and finishing a marathon are still notable feats. Even if elusive for most, they are on many people's wish list. No matter what the unimpressed say, I know firsthand finishing a marathon is "a thing."

If you had told me years ago, I would run a marathon someday, let alone many, and I would have been happy and surprised. I was like the many who deny and say, "I could never do that." When I hear that now, my response is, "Yes, you could, but?" The caution involves what I have found. The time to train, the ideal mentality, and the luck to stay healthy are sizable warnings.

I primarily agree with a young person who says they could not do it, even though it may not be why they say it. I respond by agreeing with their reservation, "When I was your age, I couldn't have run one either. I would never have had the patience to spend that amount of time out jogging." I'm not referring to the many days of necessary training because I did that as a professional athlete. But it's the patience and mind control to overcome the monotony of hours in one training run. The psychological aspect for that length of time is what I could not have handled years ago. Then, I was in a rush to get somewhere, see someone, or get something done. Now, not so much.

I suppose that is an advantage of advanced age. **At this life point, I have the mental imperturbability to tax the mind while wandering about for hours on end.**

Create Aspirations Big and Small

Step one — setting a goal. Success starts with recognizing that something worth getting is out there, and without a firm objective, the necessary vision and motivation dwindles soon.

Goals come in all sizes. Small aims are New Year's Resolutions or a daily purpose. Setting out to run a couple of miles or get two hits a game are examples. Those notions involve life pursuits that better us in the short term. The minute we don't follow through on them or fail to get them, a little heartache ensues, and achieving them provide short-term pleasure.

More ambitious targets take more allegiance. A much-desired job or scampering many miles would qualify as such. After falling short of medium-range aims, a lousy mood lasts a while. More lasting contentment arrives when we meet them.

Then, there are dreams. They require an "all in" attitude and commitment. They become ingrained in one's heart and soul. Failing to seize them hurts forever, but attaining them provides an enormous amount of self-worth and life-long joy. An example of reaching dreams is reaching the highest level you desire and running a marathon.

The point is, there are goals, and there are GOALS — the highest destinations. The "far-reachers" stretch us and are only attainable with a tremendous work ethic and dedication. Fred DeVito said, "If it doesn't challenge you, it won't change you." Striving to finish a marathon and make the Major Leagues changed me. Both endeavors fall into the GOALS category of athletic pursuits.

The critical takeaway is that energy and purpose result when one has short, medium, and long-term aspirations happening simultaneously. Most people try quick attempts, and some attempt the intermediate ones. But most people spend a lot of time thinking of their deep-seated dreams but never act on them.

Dig Deep for Courage

Step two — getting the courage to try. Once an aim is in place, you must embrace it by heading out the door. People are generally afraid to put themselves in spots where failure is a high probability. One must realize failure is an inherent part of goals, but it must not deter one. Until one dares to move on to their intention, they will never know their potential. Giving things a try is how passion develops. Many people never find their true loves because of failing to "give it a shot." Poet T.S. Eliot said, *"Only those who risk going too far can possibly find out how far one can go."* I'm sure he wasn't talking about scurrying on foot, but it speaks to moving on one's pursuits.

Discover Inspiration

Step three — gaining the preliminary knowledge. After one finds a dream and the bravery to get out the door, the next phase is finding out what it will take. Those who try to do it alone miss out on valuable knowledge and inhibit the chances of finishing. Very few can grasp the summit without knowing the means to get there. The most valuable learning comes from one's successes and failures, and the more extensive one's experience, the better. Even though some knowledge will only come with experience, available advice can save time and energy. As I advanced baseball levels, I interrogated my coaches and read about many great players to discover their "Road to the Show." Just a word or two here and there can give one a needed edge to proceed.

When it comes to running, valuable information is online. Combining the tips with a trial-and-error approach is the most straightforward path to what works. Additionally, when you encounter a fellow runner, ask them about their methods, routines, and diet. I am always on the lookout for efficient strategy and motivation to make runs flow. Other sources of knowledge and inspiration are movies, books, songs, and quotes about courage. Stories and words help with discovering the courage to keep going.

Here are some descriptions, reasons, and motivational tips that I've used for encouragement. I add in my "Two cents" after each.

"You are never too old to set another goal or to dream a new dream." C. S. Lewis

Amen to that!

"Running is a road to self-awareness and reliance — you can push yourself to extremes and learn the harsh reality of your physical and mental limitations or coast quietly down a solitary path watching the earth spin beneath your feet. Doris Brown Heritage, in every running Hall of Fame.

Doris explains the variable nature of motivation with the alternating of harsh reality and cruising. By applying strengths and overcoming weaknesses, you gain the experience to be better the next time.

"I want to compare faith to running in a race. It's hard. It requires concentration of will, energy of soul." Erik Liddell, Missionary, and Olympic Winner

It's paramount to trust the plan, yourself, and your commitment to your purpose.

"Racing teaches us to challenge ourselves. It teaches us to push beyond where we thought we could go. It helps us to find out what we are made of. This is what we do. This is what it's all about." PattiSue Plumer, Two-time Olympian

I've pushed myself many times, even though I'm not sure I went beyond where I could go, but it had to be close. I'm not sure I will ever find out who I am, but the quote sums up marathon school and runners – this is what we do, and your competition is in the mirror.

A funny one — *"No doubt a brain and some shoes are essential for marathon success. Although if it comes down to a choice, pick the shoes. More people finish with no brains than with no shoes."* Don Kardong, Journalist, Author, and Olympic Marathon Runner

I'm sure a good point is in there. If I had a dollar for every time I've quizzed my intelligence when trekking far, I would have the elusive million talked about earlier.

Another humorous explanation comes from an unlikely source, Charles Shultz — *"As a general rule, Nelson, Life is hard. But every now and then, we get to see the beauty of God's creations. And for just a moment life is beautiful... and then, life is hard again." Peanuts Cartoon*

This passage is so insightful once you substitute the word running for life. It then describes a marathon perfectly. Running is hard when the miles seem

21

forever, but at times, everything is beautiful, and you are "one" with the running gods. But, as after a festive party, a hangover follows.

To have a baseball reference here, I go to the master quote machine, Hall of Famer Yogi Berra. He reasoned, *"It gets late early out there."*

Yes, it does, Yogi. Once mile 10 or so comes, it feels like midnight, even though still a long way to go.

And two other favorites:

"Remember that guy who gave up? Neither does anyone else." **Author unknown**

"Most people never run far enough on their first wind to find out they've got a second." **William James**

Don't be either of those people!

Grow a Winning Attitude

Step four — understanding you can win even when you do not reach the ultimate. My former manager Tommy Lasorda said, "The best possible thing in baseball is winning the World Series. The second-best thing is losing the World Series." Another coaching great, John Wooden, said he felt better about some of his teams that didn't win the championship because they were closer to reaching their potential. Therein lies the point that most people miss because they only think of a winner and loser. Not everyone can be the champ, but that doesn't diminish the runners-up feat and make them losers.

So, I am not one of those coaches who say, "You can be anything you want to be." That is not realistic advice. Many who set out to run a marathon realize the 26.2 miles is out of their league. Take no shame in that awakening. It takes five months of almost daily exercise, with considerable time consumption and effort. The amount of activity can lead to health issues that deter your endgame, even with a willing heart.

Come to Play

A crucial piece to winning comes from reading about the top athletes. It's not surprising to discover they play as hard in practice as they do in games, which leads to another aspect of triumph — not taking games or individual plays off. The victor "brings it" every minute, in workouts and contests, at least as much as possible. "Gamers" play with intensity, no matter the score or situation, and when it's over, they do not make excuses. **The winner has only one regret, wishing they could have done more.**

As every competitor discovers, desires have a downside because of failure, either perceived or actual. So, how does one win when they do not attain the ultimate? Defining success in the right way is the answer. **Any effort that has changed one's life for the better equals success. You win when you give your all, even if short of the desired end.**

When an attempt to run the marathon results in any of these, you have won:

· An exercise schedule that produces a healthier lifestyle

· Going further than ever before or beyond expectations

· A routine and structure to your days

· Getting that elusive "alone time" you've been wanting or needing

· Meeting and bonding with other similar minded people

· Feeling better about oneself and more empowered to access your life's potential

· The realization your mind comes to life when you move

· Learning new things about yourself

If you drop your marathon dream but continue a runner's lifestyle, you are a winner. Any distance or schedule is a tremendous feat when it pushes you beyond what you did before. The day comes for all athletes to lower expectations once "Father Time" or "Sir Body" comes knocking. That's the nature of sports and life, but that should not deter one from continuing to exercise and look for new challenges.

A Marathon Legend Capsule

Memorable Tips

The knowledge to do it is out there, so don't leave home without it.

Imagine you are out with friends and the conversation dries up. The following may come in handy at the time or for a trivia contest you entered. Mostly, they give food for thought when out on your long runs. I give my take after each item.

- It takes approximately 55,000 strides to run a marathon. **When your weekly steps total needs a boost, it's an excellent way to go, so be sure to charge the pedometer before heading out.**

- Hitting the wall is a depletion of muscle glycogen, usually after twenty miles. **It's a high and robust barrier, which appears right in front of you without any warning, so proper preparation is the only way over it.**

- Dean Karnazes ran 50 marathons in 50 days and 50 different states, the whole USA. **So, when you begin to complain about doing one, stop, and think of "Mr. 50."**

- The "Big Six" marathons are Boston, New York, Chicago, London, Berlin, and Tokyo. **I have a way to go, but each site sounds thrilling, even without the run. If you go that far, you may as well take in the sights with the fast-foot-tour.**

- In 2018, more females entered a marathon than males in the USA. **I have nothing else to add to this one, just saying.**

- Humans are the best long-distance runners of all animals. **However, according to past results, you may have to go further than 26.2 miles to defeat a horse if you consider taking on that challenge.**

- If you want a super cool marathon, there is an annual North Pole Marathon, at least before the pandemic. **I hear it's a great place to chill out.**

Finally, if running 26.2 miles takes up too much time in your day or seems dull, the solution is simple – run faster. **I keep reminding myself of that but to no avail.**

My Story: Dream Chaser

So this is who I am

And this is all I know

And I must choose to live

For all that I can give

The spark that makes the power grow

And I will stand for my dream if I can

Symbol of my faith in who I am

Celine Dion "*Immortality***"**

Lessons of the Heart

I can't say running a marathon is more demanding than making or playing in the major leagues. Fewer than 25,000 people have ever played at that level. Yet, more than 50,000 people finished the 2019 New York City Marathon, one of many held each year. Furthermore, running involves basic movements that most people can do. Baseball requires developed physical tools and the repetition of complex fundamentals. But I have found that completing a marathon requires the same attention and athletic spirit as playing in the major leagues. I know A unique "heart" is a prerequisite to survive the ups and downs in both pastimes.

My early years of playing baseball and my bucket list item of a marathon were about "The Dream." I can trace my Major Leagues hope back to about six years old. Watching TV games helped develop it, but my wishes primarily began playing ball with my dad. After working two jobs, he never failed to say "yes" to a game of catch afterward. That loving gesture was an early life lesson for me, too. After my playing career, I wondered what it would be like to run a marathon. Times spent imagining forms the initial motivation for any significant undertaking. When the two dreams got into my heart and soul, the door opened for making them come true.

The next phase of my pursuits involved building the skills. It takes relentless practice and muscular development to keep one on the field and the track. One must develop a willingness to embrace the contests with a never-give-in attitude while knowing the will to work each day is the only chance of leapfrogging the inevitable obstacles. The baseball season is a mental and physical exam, day after day, for seven months. A marathon and training are a psychological and physical test, mile after mile, for five months and 26.2 miles. The secret to accomplishing both is to match the work ethic to the ambition's size, a challenge itself. It's worth noting, though, if getting something desired came painlessly, it was likely not a dream in the first place.

I learned from both demanding undertakings that self-doubt results. The key to overcoming skepticism and completing the mission is an optimistic life perspective. No matter how much sacrifice and failures, I had faith in it working out by making the major leagues. In a marathon, reservations about finishing come as the body and mind wither, but I trust I will have the perseverance to finish.

Lessons of the Soul

Another critical component to accomplish my dreams was convincing myself the goal was fundamental to my being. That persuasion was the needed focus and edge to look at finishing as the only alternative. Being a major league player was who I wanted to be, and a marathon runner has become who I am now. Attaining a wish rarely happens without the challenge being paramount to who one wants to be and then visualizing that result.

I also understood the importance of observing the path others took. Reading about high achieving ballplayers and runners taught me no "one-way fits all," but a relentless work ethic was the common denominator for all.

The acquired athletic philosophy also meant no offseason exists for the ballplayer and runner. A short physical and mental break came after each race and ball season, but, soon the itch to improve returned. The "Eye of the Tiger" temperament would grip me, along with a pledge to give my all again. The love of what one does gets them back out on the trail and the ball diamond before long. Sure, sometimes, I do not feel like doing the work, but doing it anyway is the "fight" I know is necessary to win.

Finally, the belief that I can do better than the previous marathon or ball season is motivation. Pushing for daily discipline and an unwavering belief that the end is worth the means is what an athlete is. Game on, let's go!

29

3
The Commitment Mindset

A Dream

Why do I not feel better? I just had the game of my life and one I dreamed of forever. I leave the clubhouse, and no one is there to greet me – no family, friends. It is such an empty feeling.

I wake and mull over its meaning. This night tale explains joy is absent when one has no one to share their life experiences. Life is gratifying when we see the necessity and beauty of others.

"It's easy to get outside yourself when you're thinking about someone else."

Christopher McDougall *Born to Run*

Yes, Christopher, often, it is advantageous to leave one's ego at the front door.

The success trail is demoralizing at times. Here are the critical secrets to persevere.

Stairway to success:

5. A prominent cause

6. Accountability

Step Higher

Here's the thing. The setting of goals is not the hard part. Consider how often you tell yourself, "Tomorrow I will start such and such," only never to chase it. Likewise, what usually happens, we begin a pursuit, but it fades away over time.

Step five — devising a deep-seated purpose for driving motivation. The goal and start of it begin the process, but **a compelling reason or reasons give aspirations a real chance.** The establishment of a profound "why" is a game-changer, and without it, the attempt will end the way of most New Year's Resolutions. I can think of many times in my life I set out to do something, only to see my commitment to it waver soon after. It's critical to explore your reasons for doing it, write them, and add to it as you go. **Refer to the mission statement whenever you need to regain momentum, which is usually often.**

Here are some reasons for engagement, and although some may seem simple, they are influential when you believe them.

Because:

* I have to!

* It is who I aspire to be.

* No one thought I could.

* I was tired of "same old, same old."

* I needed a new direction.

* It looked fun.

* I wanted a life reset.

* I sought time to myself.

* A friend asked me to join them.

* I loved being around the activity and people.

* I believed in the cause.

* Others depended on me.

* It was always a dream of mine.

* The challenge was staring me down.

* Mike did it.

How can you not go through with a venture if you say, "Because I have to." Any of the above is sufficient motivation, and often, there are many reasons for ambition. Another of my go-to favorites comes from the Blues Brothers movie, "We're on a mission from God." I substitute "I'm," and it becomes a practical reason for all life undertakings.

Follow your Heroes!

Of all the above reasons for doing something, a dominant one is the last one, "So and so does it." A considerable life motivational force comes from doing things people we admire do. Sometimes, all it takes to convince us to try something is seeing another's life and thinking, "That's for me." I had major league baseball heroes growing up, and they made me say, "I want to be like them." One should always be on the lookout for people to follow and attempt to walk in their footsteps. My first thoughts of running go back to the 1968 Olympics and to distance runner Jim Ryun. I can see him in my mind to this day, and memories of him, and athletes like Jesse Owens, give me pride in being a runner.

Respond to the Inevitable Queries

Reaching a strenuous goal, like a marathon, requires solid motives because the following questions will inhabit your mind:

"Why am I doing this while my friends are watching the ballgame?"

"Why keep working so hard with this pain?"

"Why not take the day off instead?"

"Why does it seem like I never improve?"

"Why is it not OK to stop and settle for less?"

Running a marathon is an exercise in being as comfortable as possible when uncomfortable, and **those who extend beyond their comfort level achieve more than those who cannot.** A developed powerful "why" is what helps you respond to the why questions.

Go Beyond Yourself

Having reasons and backing is excellent, but you may still need more. Once I came across the line in the book *Born to Run* at the beginning of this chapter, it changed my perspective. I always knew including others was significant but didn't always do it. I now do what I can to enhance other lives, and the pleasure that comes from it is immense. **Striving for goals is personally rewarding but doing something beyond oneself makes it captivating.**

Some professional athletes point to the sky or at their teammates after a successful outcome. They dedicate their play to someone or something besides themselves, and putting one's focus on a game-changing purpose is the beginning of becoming a HERO. Not only are you helping those in need, but it is powerful motivation the moment you contemplate slacking or stopping. For something as demanding as a marathon, the extra inspiration is a savior. **A commitment beyond you and to something deep in your heart motivates as no other thing can.**

Create Purpose

It's obvious why and who you want to run for at some life moments, while other times, you may have to search for a reason. Once you dedicate your run, tell others about the attention and financial help you intend to bring to the cause. Announce your intention to social media friends, too, if that is your thing. Your purpose may be an ill friend, someone going through a tough time, a charity, or a combination of things. Once again, **the push one gets from heartfelt motives makes a difference, and knowing you play a role in helping others is humbling.**

The cause I have chosen for the last number of years is the Kids of St. Jude's Hospital. Those youngsters have challenges that no kid deserves. It's the perfect cause for me, seeing how I have worked with youth athletes for the past thirty years. Anything I can do to help them have a bright future gives satisfaction. Thoughts of the kids and donors give me a second, third, and fourth wind when considering stopping. I pray for the kids and call to mind what the donors have meant to me. It's a fun mental exercise to recollect the sharing of smiles, laughs, tears, friendship, work, interests, and family times.

Most marathons have a Run for Charity program to support, and raising a specified amount may include the entrée fee for the race. You can also raise money on your own and donate it to your charity of choice. The cool thing is many friends are willing to help when they see you are putting in an unreal effort of 26.2 miles and doing it for others. People's donations for each mile on race day adds motivation not to stop. Even 50 cents or one dollar per mile adds up when you multiply it by many miles and friends.

Have an Attitude of Accountability

Step six — being accountable. Now that you've established a goal and purpose, one must set the stage to remain faithful to the process. Marathon training accountability is either you are doing the daily suggested miles on the training schedule or not. But it is never that easy, and **you must have mechanisms in place to hold yourself loyal to the cause.** Difficult periods lay ahead, and the following aid in self-accountability.

* Study your mission statement, intent, and process.

* List your strengths and weaknesses and how you can enhance the former and limit the latter.

* Setup and examine every aspect of your daily, weekly, and monthly plan.

* Keep things as simple as possible. Top athletes strive to improve daily and let their statistics come as they may.

* Prepare the mind with the perspective, "To be a finisher, one must train like one."

* Avoid excuse-making by recognizing it's on you!

Gather Support

Along with self-accountability, it helps to be responsible to others. Elite athletes have their "team," people who aid them with the highest chances of success. They have a conditioning coach, a nutritionist, a psychologist, and a skills coach. Those are excessive for the amateur, but you should address each area, too. You may reason help is unnecessary, but **going it alone is a recipe for loneliness. Even if you get to the end on your own, the joy will be less.** To enjoy the adventure to the fullest, invite family and friends to engage in your fight. The support puts you in a position to make it. Once in place, you now have "your team" as the pros have, and it will bring comfort to you and them. At every opportunity, thank them for the assistance and include them in your celebrations. The gratitude you show often comes back to you later.

Here are some things to be sure to get help with:

· **Proper nutrition.** Healthy eating is on you, but it helps to have roommates, friends, and family aide you in a nutritious diet.

· **Cross-training exercise**. If not a trainer, at the least, research effective methods to maintain the highest condition level possible.

· **The mental game.** It never hurts to ask those close to you to help you stay positive. Reading about elite athletes, in particular, those who overcame the odds, is priceless motivation, too.

· **Skill enhancement.** It's essential to keep up with the latest training advice, and many runner's websites offer invaluable tips and support. The most enthusiastic runners may want to find a coach or a team.

A Marathon Legend Capsule

Hero Among Heroes

It's essential in life to look for and follow role models.

Who is the first person who comes to mind when thinking of a marathon? Below is mine, and there's a good chance your answer will determine your age.

It's late summer 1972, and I am entering my freshman year of college at the impressionable age of 18. As for the whole world, my attention is on the Olympic Games in Munich, Germany. Two events affect me beyond the ordinary. First, with Israeli athletes and coaches' tragic massacre, naivete left me, at least in the sports arena. From that time on, I realized sports were not separate from the real world. I may have sensed that from watching the plight of Muhammad Ali and the scorn he took from being unwilling to enter the draft, but the Olympic heartbreak drove the point home.

Second, those Olympics were the first time I paid attention to the Marathon. I probably could not have told you how many miles it was, but I knew it was more than I ever cared to run. However, I would not doubt that my one-day ambition of running a marathon came from watching the American Frank Shorter win it. To this day, as mentioned, when I think of marathon runners, my mind goes to Frank Shorter.

Having since read about the remarkable runner and man, I feel honored to have run many marathons, although not at his level, of course. Of considerable interest was reading about him entering the Olympic stadium in 1972 with thousands of people not applauding him for winning. It turns out, an imposter had jumped in ahead of him, and the fans unknowingly cheered the cheater, thinking he was the leader and winner. As if that wasn't bad enough, Frank Shorter finished second in the 1976 Olympics. The thing is, the winner turned out to be a runner who was part of the illegal doping scandal by the East Germans. It's an example of how sports and life can be bittersweet at times, and one must learn to roll with the punches, as they say. As also said, "Cheaters never win, and winners never cheat."

Frank Shorter, among others, had a huge role in starting the distance running boom in the United States, so thanks to him, marathons are widespread now. It's hard not to be inspired by greatness, and Shorter is in that category.

My Story: Why I Run

Don't let the old man in, I wanna leave this alone

Can't leave it up to him, he's knocking on my door

And I knew all of my life, that someday it would end

Get up and go outside, don't let the old man in

Toby Keith *"Don't Let the Old Man In"*

High Stepping with Purpose

An example of using life for gaining purpose came one day for me. While out running, what else, a call came. To say it stopped me in my tracks with tears is an understatement. It was one of my best friends on the other end without the usual enthusiasm in his voice. One dreaded word – leukemia. My thought is, "No way this is happening."

My marathon training became more manageable after that call. From that day forward, whenever my mind or body wanted to quit, I pictured what my friend was going through. I realized a little hurting from exercise was nothing, and his situation helped me through the challenging periods. A couple of years later, the day before I ran a marathon, my friend competed in the 5K. Yes, tears again, this time of joy. He has been an inspiration to me and many,

Eric Liddle, an Olympian and missionary of Chariots of Fire movie fame had a powerful reason to run. He said,

41

"I believe God made me for a purpose, but he also made me fast. And when I run, I feel His pleasure." My "why" is not as purposeful as Eric Liddle's, but I also know it adds meaning to my life. I believe my vision of running marathons for many more years is indispensable to my happiness. That may seem drastic, but every significant target ties into self-satisfaction and pride. When one's self-worth is on the line, the more one will strive to get the job done.

Often, I get the query, "Why do you run marathons?" I'm sure they want to add, "At your age," but don't." My smart-aleck answer is one I keep to myself, "Because I can." That response, although lighthearted, has truth behind it. I believe that things you can do, you should if the enjoyment of doing them is present. I realize how fortunate I've been to have a body that has held up over time.

My non-wise guy's answer lies in wanting to look at myself as I always have – as an athlete. It is hard to accept how time tries to prevent me from being young again. As Pink Floyd puts it in "Time,"

"And then one day you find ten years have got behind you

No one told you when to run, you missed the starting gun"

Life goes fast, so I guess by moving forward and far, I'm trying to slow it some. I can't stop ten years from going by, but I can run to make sure not to miss the starting gun! Running marathons is a way of slowing life, being in the moment, and feeling like I'm on the big stage again.

A Timely Mindset

Many questions pop up as I consider time, and it's pivotal to stay attentive and accountable to them. Using one's time wisely is a prerequisite if one wishes to accomplish a project and be happy about the time spent. The following quiz holds me accountable to time:

* Where has the time gone? **I'm 67 but feel like a kid. I realize I haven't done enough in this life, and with so much more to do, I must keep moving.**

* I know it flies, but why do I continue to waste it? **Like all athletes, I must improve at being "in the moment."**

* Can it slow? **Yes, but only in the rare moments I've "won the day."**

* Has my time come and gone? **Ha, as long as I keep on the move, my time is now.**

* Is tomorrow guaranteed? **No, I need to live as if this is my last day.**

* Should I give others more of my time? **Yes, and start today.**

* Is time on my side? **As much as anyone else's.**

* Does it heal all wounds? **To a degree, but I have hesitancy about that when every inch of me hurts at mile 17.**

And an athlete cannot talk about time without mentioning the words, "Game Time."

Inspiration

Research studies also give many convincing reasons to run and be physically active. The one that motivates me the most is why I recommend people run – the mental stimulation it creates. Whenever I get into a mental rut and the fruitful ideas dry up, movement on foot makes my brain thrust into a higher gear. Exercise brings out my cerebral functioning, as it helps me think, imagine, create, love, pray, reminisce, hope, and feel alive.

Many great ideas come while moving that fail to show up sitting and writing. If you read things here that inspire you more than usual, a good chance it cropped up when I was on the trail. I know the day I stop writing is the day I stop running. No, I mean the day I stop running is the day I stop writing. I do intend both. Many people use ideas to motivate them to move. I use movement to inspire thought.

Another reason to move is life becomes overwhelming, which happens for everyone, and my release is jogging. I'm always amazed at how it helps slow things and reorient my life. The greatest minds in our world should join a running club, so our problems may have solutions.

Defying aging, new ideas, and the tension release are excellent reasons. For another, I refer to an Ozzie Osbourne song, "And the truth is I don't want to die an ordinary man." Amen, even though he is not someone I ever dreamed of quoting.

Tongue in Cheek Reasons I run

As if the above is not reason enough, the following work to various degrees to keep me heading out the door.

How many people my age can do this, or any age, for that matter? **One should take pride in what they do well.**

What's a few hours of my time when there are so many hours in a life? **A realization that comes with age, I suppose.**

Would I instead want to be sitting at home doing nothing? **Something to do is better than nothing or household chores.**

I must get back home anyway; I may as well get there faster. **Taxi and Uber drivers do not want sweaty people in their cars.**

Use it or lose it! **That is my philosophy!**

Will I feel better by keep going or quitting? **Simple answer there.**

I am who I am. **Peace of mind comes from having and living up to the identity you want for yourself.**

Imagine how good I'll feel after completing the day's goal. **Meeting daily ambitions build character.**

4
The Planning Mindset

A Dream

I am super excited at the beginning of the marathon. I tear out of the gate and lead the race after five miles. Could it be my time? Uh oh, I realize I have tons of miles to go, and my energy already zapped. What to do now?

Another panicky nightmare whose meaning is self-explanatory. To begin without a game plan results in frustration, more work, and failure.

"It's what you learn after knowing it all that counts."

John Wooden

Yes, Coach, there is always so much more to learn.

With the initial procedures set, the success trail requires precise implementation.

Stairway to success:

7. A game plan

8. A routine

9. Knowing one's limitations

Have a Road Map

One of my regrets is not having a consistent, intelligent plan in my baseball career. Working smarter would have been more productive. I changed things frequently, which led to inconsistency, and found out the hard way "Practice does not make perfect; perfect practice makes perfect." Furthermore, ignorance of the fundamentals led to overworking to the point of near exhaustion. Unfortunately, there are no do-overs.

As for running, the good news is you know how to run, and anything faster than walking fits the bill. It's not that walking is a bad thing, except the objective, in this case, is to run a marathon. If you haven't been active, don't get discouraged; it's OK to take things slow before the long climb up the marathon mountain.

Step seven — forming a game plan. The design is an ongoing formula of using what works and discarding what doesn't. A blueprint helps avoid the frequent deliberation of, "If I only knew then what I now know," and stresses the importance of details.

Employ a Start-up Scheme

Whether a frequent runner or one just getting started, the following is a good start, so one does not overdo it and burn out soon after.

* Start today and run a block or two, a mile, 5 minutes, whatever is comfortable. Use the time to find "your" pace, the speed that seems you are light on your feet and not pushing it. If you get to the point where you cannot talk or sing a lyric without gasping, slow it up. It should be fun, knowing the unavoidable grind will come later. If you must walk or alternate it with running initially, that is OK. Finding a well-populated trail is a good plan because it makes you a member of the runner's community, and seeing others moving along inspires you not to let up.

* Add a little distance or a few minutes each time out, even if it's only a bit of either, for at least three days a week. Some soreness may ensue, but that is a sign that you are on your way to fitness. The athletic code, something to know, says you can play with pain, not with an injury. Also, trust me on this; the best way to get rid of achiness is by getting back up and moving. You will find out the body has a unique ability to recover, the result of using it. Even at a slower pace, the movement eases pain sooner than not moving. If you stay inactive over every pain, you won't leave the house very often. Of course, consult a doctor when pain persists for an extended period.

* Be sure to celebrate any extra distance and minutes you gain. Taking joy from the little achievements along the way should be a priority. **Many athletes burn out from dwelling on the setbacks and not rejoicing the small wins.**

* Get to the point where you have the urge to run at least every other day. It may take a while to develop a running

fever, so be patient and not discouraged. If you must force yourself to run and dread it, your goal will end before you have the chance to fall in love with it. You must understand **it takes time for habits to form.**

* Once hooked on the exercise and the five-mile mark is doable, find a marathon training guide online. The program will map out your next 20 weeks or so of training. For first-time marathoners and those not out for a designated finish time, go with the beginner schedule. Those ready for more of a test can try the intermediate program but tread lightly, and you can always revert to the beginner one if it proves too much. If you decide to go for a lesser distance, find the appropriate training schedule.

* You are now ready to tell your family and associates of your endgame. Most will encourage you, and some may distrust you can do it, but both reactions help with motivation. **If you haven't discovered this already, know that the doubters are a top source of incentive.**

* Keep in mind training takes a substantial amount of time. Four or five months of sometimes intense exercise is required. **It will feel as though running runs your life, pun intended.** If you are unwilling or do not have four or five days a week, you may want to put your target at less than a marathon.

* Off days are a necessary part of the training. **When the schedule calls for a day of rest, be sure and take it.**

* Find a cross-training exercise to do on your non-running days. I have gone some years without much strength work but regretted it at about mile 17. Bike riding, leg-

strengthening workouts, yoga, Pilates, and stair-climbing are some possibilities. Also, **power-building exercises have value in adding discipline, focus, and stimulus.**

* At this point, **you are ready to scout around for a marathon, the early training highlight.** Be sure to consider the following when choosing:

· How far from home you want to travel? **Many factors to consider when going far from home.**

· What is the best time of year to train? **Working around one's life, work schedule, and weather can make that tricky.**

· Affordability? **A wide range of marathon entry fees and travel costs exist.**

· How big of a crowd are you comfortable being around? **Big marathons mean lots and lots of people.**

· Can some family or friends attend? **Psychological and physical support is beneficial, so go alone only as a last resort.**

Finally, many race reviews will be online, and it's a good idea to read them to get a better picture of each considered marathon.

Get Hooked

The marathon choices are many, with events coming in all sizes. Notice the word event. Marathons are more than a race with the many festivities surrounding them. The coolest thing is the excitement that comes with the big marathons makes you feel like a big-time athlete. The New York, Chicago, Las Vegas, and Hawaii marathons I've run are unforgettable. Be aware the top marathons require signing up many months before, and you must join a lottery and hope to get in it. It's conducive to have a backup option or two in case.

As implied, it is exciting to research races. It was not hard for me to get hooked on the New York City marathon upon searching. One review says:

"8 miles in, you are graced with the most spectacular view of the New York Harbor, city skyline (Statue of Liberty), and the mass of the running community." **That's what I'm talking about!**

And even better:

"Coming off the Queensboro Bridge and onto First Avenue is perhaps the most thrilling experience in marathoning. The crowds are huge, and it feels like you're running through a wall of sound." **After reading that, I was "Hooked" and "Pumped" for sure.** Fortunately, I was a winning selection in the lottery. No turning back after that, I went "Big Apple" chasing.

* Once you have a marathon spot, read about it from time to time to get a good picture of it in your head. Find

photos of the course, visualize yourself on it, and crossing the finish line. The winning athlete knows **overcoming any tough encounter involves seeing yourself do it repeatedly.**

Train with a Routine

Step eight – having a routine. Most high-level athletes' have a daily schedule of getting up, eating, working out, and going to bed. They have demanding repetitive behavior with music choices, leaving for games precisely, and talking to the same people. They fear that any little thing out of its normal rhythm will affect their performance.

Superstition is not good, but regularity brings reassurance, and a set method of attack is a source of willpower and self-control. The discipline brings confidence and calms the mind during complications, and those with command do not panic and find faith in self and strategy.

People are creatures of habit, and consistency works best in training. Here are some "routine" tips that help keep you on track:

* Run the same days each week, along with a regular long-run day.

* Head out the door at a consistent time each day. The consistency brings self-assurance and provides the time to regain energy before the next outing.

* Learn which foods to eat before and after that settle well and are beneficial for stamina and recovery.

* Find a few enjoyable running trails.

* Prepare the same way before, including the clothing that gives you some "swagger."

* Use the same pattern in your cool-down period.

* Trust the power of sameness.

Each athlete's routine differs, and the search for it is an ongoing one with no one way fitting all. With distance running, the food, stretching, and cross-training exercises are unique to each runner. Reading and talking with other runners to find the best methods can find necessary consistency. To go without a routine and "wing it" brings stress and days you may not leave the house. An added benefit is the proper procedures before and after pays off with smoother runs and sleeping well. Most beneficial, **executing a steady practice will bring a disciplined mind and one's maximum effort.**

Stay within Yourself

Step nine — knowing one's limitations. At some point, you can decide how vital finishing under a specific time. When that is your intention, a more calculated pace must be in your plan, which brings us to the next ingredient for success. It takes an honest assessment of self to know your capabilities. It's hard for the athlete who has lived by the motto, "can't is a dirty word," but there are times when they must admit, "No, not this time." The competitor always thinks "more," but that may not be the best approach. Discipline is critical to stay within oneself as the weeks pass. As you develop your strategy and routine, pay attention to your psyche and body to know when to push and back off. **Remember, diving into the deep waters without a life preserver may leave one flailing.** For those who have little athletic history, jumping to the marathon level may not be wise. Instead, shoot for a 5K, then 10K, and proceed to the half before a full marathon.

I pay attention to the body's signals to know what it can and can't do each run. I would love to run sub-4-hour marathons, but at this stage, I know those days are long gone, so a constant recognition of a slower pace is necessary. The athlete must learn their strengths and weaknesses to get the most out of themselves without putting them in danger of overexertion, which you pay for with injury or missed practice. That is not to say one should not push themselves but staying within one's limits is critical over the long haul.

A Marathon Legend Capsule

K.V. Does It

Here's the plan. Do something no one has ever done. Sounds simple, right?

The beginning of extraordinary events and the first people to do something is always fascinating, especially when years of "denying the opportunity" took place. Such is the story of the women's Marathon and the path to it becoming an Olympic sport. A big part of that coming to fruition began in the 1960s. In the 1966 Boston Marathon, a Roberta "Bobby" Gibb jumped into the race right after the start because women were not allowed, and she finished. The following year she ran from the start and was yanked off the course near the finish line.

In that 1967 race, a remarkable story took place as a runner named K.V. Switzer ran and finished the race. Kathrine Switzer didn't try to hide her identity on the race day but entered with initials and received an entry. Her story of the race was fascinating. She noted how many runners were happy to have a woman among them, even though most doubted she would run the whole way. That inviting spirit didn't extend to all the race officials as one physically fought to have her removed during the run. With help from friends, she was able to remain in the race.

As indicated, being a "first" requires struggle. Kathryn knew after the altercation that she "had to" finish because the reason women were not allowed to run marathons was "They were not physically capable of it." That philosophy is funny to think of now with the number of women doing them, but the prevailing thought then. She finished with unbelievably torn-up feet but made a statement for all to see. To dispel the myth, she invoked the competitor's mindset of not quitting.

Thanks to Katherine Switzer and many other amazing women, the first all-women Marathon occurred in Germany six years later. Kathrine Switzer became instrumental in organizing women's running events in subsequent years. As they became more prominent, it led to the women's marathon in the 1984 Olympic Games and every Olympics after that.

This tale of firsts reinforces three lessons I've hinted upon:

- Nothing worthwhile comes easily.
- Quitting cannot be an option.
- One should never underestimate the determination of the myth-breaker.

My Story: Freedom Road

So When You Feel Like Hope Is Gone

Look Inside You And Be Strong

And You'll Finally See The Truth

That A Hero Lies In You

Mariah Carey "Hero"

Smart Steps

Running is 90% mental, and the other 50% is physical. Baseball fans will know that calculation is an infringement on another quote by the great Hall of Famer, Yogi Berra. He is correct in that a routine is not just for physical training but also the cerebral part. The following conceptual habit gets me to a destination where the exertion is worth it. It isn't something I set out to do, but it often happens this way. I hope this can happen for you too. It's another desired result – peace of mind, even if it is temporary.

Shedding the Riffraff

It must be getting early, clocks are running late

Paint-by-number morning sky looks so phony

Dawn is breaking everywhere, light a candle, curse the glare

Draw the curtains, I don't care 'cause it's alright

I will get by

The Grateful Dead *"A Touch of Grey"*

I spend the first few miles reviewing recent annoying events and people. Incidents like the idiot driver who cut me off in traffic so he could get to his destination seconds sooner. And the ten-year-old ballplayer who looks at me as if I never played the game in my life when I suggest a way to play. Then, the bothersome kid called me "Dude," and the adult addressed me as "Bro." Having been a youth sports coach for 30 years, I have a lot of patience. But, someone over sixty years old (me) should get a little more respect than "Dude" or "Bro." Just me, I guess. Along with my disgust, I consider the ways I wish I would have responded. I plan, so I'm ready the next time.

Each week, a new set of similar gripes occupy the first phase of a run. After a few miles, I laugh and realize graver life issues exist than a few slights. I start to flush them out of my memory and understand they were not that big a deal in the first place. I recognize others get disrespected much worse. Learning to handle negativity is decisive for an athlete, and even more so in the internet age.

With those sensitivities behind me, I turn to Anger Management Class 2. Vital issues come to mind like, "How the f--- did our country and the world get in this state of disarray?" And "I know there is a God, but what happened to our humanity?" And another worldly one, "How can anyone deny climate change or call something so evil a Hoax?" and, "Will the world return to normal again, not that it ever was?" My disillusion comes with no answers, but time and I march on.

The Relinquishing

I can't be free with what's locked inside of me

If there was a key you took it in your hand

There's no wrong or right but I'm sure there's good and bad

The questions linger overhead

Pearl Jam *"Thumbing My Way"*

After dwelling on personal and world problems, I need to jump into Lake Michigan to rinse off. Seeing how I am not much of a swimmer and not intending to enter the Ironman Triathlon, I keep going. I realize things could be worse, and people much brighter than I do not have the answers, either.

I begin to put the deliberations behind me, and the transformation miles start. My worries, gripes, and irritations leave with each step, and beautiful imaginings arrive. I summon up Eddie Vedder singing, "Oh, I'm a lucky man to count on both hands the ones I love." Louis Armstrong's song, "What a Wonderful World," and the Beatles, "All the lovely people." I now notice the beautiful surroundings and people. I see my potential on the horizon.

I think of an interview I heard with a guy in his 90" s, not an old "Dude" or a "Bro," but a wise Gentleman. Asked if he wished he would have accomplished more in his life, he responded, "No, I wish I would have loved more."

Therein is the secret to happiness – loving more and understanding it's not so much what you do; it's how you do it.

As the mind unburdens, I move into the prayer part of my run. I do not pray for an easy run but for the strength to endure a difficult one. I pray for the capacity to make the moves to be a better person. I appeal to a higher being to help me be there for those who need me.

Reaching the Destination

No matter how cold the winter, there's a springtime ahead

I'm thumbing my way back to heaven

I wish that I could hold you, I wish that I had

Thinking 'bout heaven

Pearl Jam – *"Thumbing My Way"*

Near the end, and even though exhaustion is creeping in, freedom shows up. The mind has come to a peaceful state, and nothing can deter this sensation. For example, a car runs a red light and almost clips me, and I smile and wave no big deal. I get a text from a parent stating my student got exactly zero hits over the weekend. I shake it off, realizing it is the nature of competition. I respond with, "Hang in there; things will get better the next game." I arrive home and discover the water heater blew out. For complete proof of my tranquility, I shrug it off, "That's OK, I love cold showers, and it gives me a chance to clean up the basement." I must be at peace because this would typically elicit a profane, disgusting response. But there is no dispute; harmony has come.

Is this the "Runner's High" I have read about. Whatever? Satisfaction and serenity are welcome, and I am ready to take on another week with renewed enthusiasm. I am determined not to let the little things bother me.

You may now see how running can help find the sanity everyone desires. To un-clutter the mind and have freedom makes the grind worthwhile. It is a fleeting, glorious moment that passes when I think of all the things I have to do the upcoming week or after watching the nightly news. Oh well, although short-lived, I am grateful to have a way of passing my worries away and renewing my spirit.

5

The Health Mindset

If Only a Dream

In one of my marathons, I was crushing it. 5,10,15, 20, and even 25 miles went by like a cool breeze on a beautiful summer day. Then, as athletes often get, an "Are you kidding me?" moment arrives. A thunderbolt out of nowhere, and I am sick as a dog. I had to walk the entire last mile, point two. It's astounding to think 20 minutes could feel much longer than the four hours before.

That is a long way of saying never to take health for granted. The physical nature of sports takes a toll on every athlete, sooner or later.

"You don't have to run faster than the bear. You have to run faster than the other guy running from the bear." **An unknown author**

That is a hilarious, dire take on safety, but being fearful can bring out one's best.

Getting stalled on the success trail deters progress, so one must avoid that situation.

Stairway to success:

10. Health

Beware of Danger – It's Everywhere

In the book *Born to Run*, a fascinating line stands out, "The real mutants are the runners who don't get injured." Great point! I never considered myself a mutant, but hey, it works for me. Not that I haven't had my share of athletic injuries, but for the most part, I've been a lucky mutation so far.

Step ten — remaining healthy. In athletics, that's staying injury-free, which starts with being attentive to the body. Any weak spot, muscle or joint, will show up painfully. It's pivotal to take proper care of the aches, even minor ones, and when you don't, they can turn into "showstoppers." A healthy lifestyle is the first prerequisite for health with proper nutrition, rest, and moderation with everything necessary actions. Remaining healthy is the way to earn the adjective "experienced" for an athlete.

Before training, athletes should learn the common injuries and ways to avoid them. Even though one deems running as a non-contact sport, it is precisely that. The continual pounding on the ground makes it so and leads to excessive danger points. Overuse injuries are typical for hard-working athletes and runners, with developmental delays inhibiting the chances of finishing.

The most prominent running dangers are various lower-body ailments, including stress fractures and shin splints, along with dehydration and hypoglycemia. The last two names alone indicate they are no fun. I've had both, and yes, they suck. Both dangers are more likely in the longer runs, but I have faced them on runs that were not the longest, too. Even though 9, 11, or 13 miles may seem minor compared to 26.2, I did what I know an athlete should not do. **I took the easier opponents (mileage amount) too casually by not eating or hydrating enough.** I've been fortunate so far to have stayed away from any significant leg issues. It's critical to take care of any leg ache with proper care immediately after runs, as alluded. Runners should not be surprised that ice and Ibuprofen become two of their best friends.

One of my worst mistakes was a post-run recovery drink. One year, I formed a bad habit of drinking soda after long runs, which led to kidney stones. The pain was immense as one would expect, and the sting of my stupidity hurt almost as much.

Know the Trail Menaces

Many significant hazards await the runner. Moving vehicles, which I've had almost collisions with every type, are uppermost on the list. To get to my usual path, I must run a mile through Chicago's streets. The first thing to know, big-city drivers are unpredictable, to put it kindly. **One early or late move before or after a red light or stop sign can be deadly, no exaggeration, so patience and instincts are crucial.**

My son, also a runner, warns me, "Cars hate runners, and runners hate automobiles, but everybody hates bikers." There is no disrespect intended to the bicyclists out there, but yes, the bikers fly by and believe it is their world. It's not the same as getting hit by a truck or car, but damage can occur to both you and the cyclist.

Runners should not trust anything on wheels, including people on rolling and motorized boards. Be aware of your surroundings because moving devices can appear out of nowhere, which means being mindful of what's behind them, too. Another danger is alleyways. Drivers may honk as they get to the walkway, but that only gives you notice the last sound heard before panic or collision was a horn.

As if those are not enough, the most common danger is the most innocent looking — the path itself. The second you take the trail too casually, and I mean second, it finds a way to remind you that it has the power to trip you up.

Remember, any delay in training costs momentum, and every training mile is valuable. Remaining fit and safe is a work in progress with experience as the best teacher. The ideal philosophy is to air on the side of caution and prepare for every eventuality. **It's never fun to learn the hard way how to remain healthy.** Write or take mental notes of what works to not make the same mistakes in the future.

Maintain Healthy Actions

⚠ Have comfortable, sturdy, and worn-in shoes. Fortunately, I have never had trouble with any shoes. Old, new, lightweight, heavy, cheap, expensive, I suspect I could run barefoot if the surface were fine, but I don't ever plan to find that out. But that's just me. My reason for a reliable pair of shoes is for stepping on unseen stones. They hurt with worn shoes more than with new ones, and of course, glass can cut through worn soles.

For most, **get the right shoes!** If you suffer from continual foot, leg, knee, hip, or ankle pain, changing

65

shoes may be a solution. With persistent pain, consult with an orthopedic doctor or running specialist to get fitted for shoes. If it turns out to be the way you run, that is a whole other issue. Reading about the correct techniques for distance runners can be of benefit. **But "If it ain't broke, there is nothing to fix" is the athletic philosophy when having only occasional discomfort**. Every person's body has unique actions, so altering your stride or landing to follow the latest advice may not be helpful or wise.

A blister can set you back a spell, so do not trust shoes until broken in completely. For the same reason, a well-fitted pair of socks is another essential.

⚠ Have a cautionary philosophy. Walking, stopping, and stretching are OK and could be what's necessary. **You may think you're failing by walking or quitting, but it is the right thing for substantial discomfort**. Sometimes, after a short pause, I continue and am fine the rest of the way. When I come upon a hill that seems to be a mountain, I draw the line and walk up quickly. Once I know I'm at my absolute limit of miles for the day, though less than planned, I stop. Slacking a little in training is wise when health is in jeopardy. I summon up the literal quote, "It's a marathon, not a sprint."

If you have any lightheadedness, it is exceedingly foolish to keep going. That danger is reason to stop and live to fight another day! Also, know imbibing too much alcohol the night before is not the type of hydration recommended. An even worse hangover may be right around the corner if you think running is the cure for a hangover.

The only time I may try to push beyond high discomfort is on the marathon day itself, but not beyond common sense.

⚠ Take treadmill running seriously. The machines are not entirely safe, either, even though it's a smooth surface. The exercise device can be hazardous if your concentration on pace is lacking. The boredom is troubling, too, especially with never getting anywhere or passing anyone; I chuckle. Of course, treadmills allow you to avoid many of the hazards listed here, but that takes away some of the fun challenges, too. It's always beneficial to practice as you play, and unless the marathon is on a treadmill, avoid it when a healthy option exists. Another consideration is that with less air resistance than outside, one must run further on a treadmill for the same workout level.

⚠ Pack lightly, but pack. Bring enough drinks and light snacks, or get them along the way, for longer distance runs. Other things for longer treks are anti-chafe cream, ibuprofen, and analgesic spray. Also, you may want to consider Kleenex, paper towels, sunglasses, and lifesavers (the hard candy). I joke, but the concept and taste help. An official runner's belt is a worthwhile investment to carry items and will not weigh you down.

⚠Find a legitimate trail, and **do not just wing your route. Uneven surfaces make it hazardous, and unknown areas can be risky**. "Lost" is not a comfortable feeling, and decisions on where to go exhaust energy. Softer surfaces help with the landing shock but always choose even over texture. Most marathons are on paved streets, so it can be a plus to prepare for the hard surface.

For street running, take non-busy ones when choosing and take safe, smooth roads over sidewalks. The latter's cracks are a stubbed toe ready to happen, at the least. (More on that later.) And, do not trust curbs — they are often slippery and are higher than you think, especially when the legs are heavy.

⚠ Beware of climate change. Check the weather before going because change can come quickly. **Mother Nature is unpredictable and furious some days**. Wear or pack rainproof clothing for a high chance of rain if you head out. (More on this hazard later, too.)

⚠ Power up. Don't leave home without a charged cell phone, even though you may want to get away from all communication devices. Many things can go wrong, and **your phone can be your lifeline**. It is never a bad idea to share your route with someone beforehand, too.

⚠ Nighttime running is inadvisable. If no other alternatives, only travel in well-lit, familiar areas. It's critical to **wear suitable colored clothing and have a light for you to see, along with glow-in-the-dark lights for others to know of your presence. It's beyond urgent to be visible, so investing in wearable body lights for night running is advised**. Bright, reflective colors on gloomy days and darkness are effective. Conversely, on sunny days, dark-colored clothing stands out.

Avoid the Unseen

⚠ Beware of the mentioned and alarming hypoglycemia and dehydration. Never neglect or forget the importance of proper eating and drinking. A lack of energy will lead to an early end and a terrible hangover, leading to missed training runs. However, do not go overboard, even if the items seem healthy and recommended. Another of my athletic sons learned the hard way and ruined his post-run enjoyment after a fabulous run. He drank two energy drinks immediately after imbibing it on the run, and it was too much. Overloading anything is not a good idea.

The immediate days before the extended runs should include carbohydrate loading. That is a fancy way of saying to eat pasta, fruits, and vegetables. Carb-loading is elemental for endurance athletes, whose bodies need more energy. Carbs help with less fatigue, better performance, and recovery. I eat more than ordinary the day before treks of at least 15 miles, and the days before the marathon, I pack in the calories, knowing their value for a run of such magnitude. Once again, **eating and hydrating too little is a recipe for trouble**. Overeating to the "bloating" point is not good either, but I recommend a little more than less when in doubt. One can and should find a list of healthy foods and drinks online with eating another of those trial-and-error processes.

For first-timers, do not fall for the trap of assuming, "Because I run a lot, I can eat whatever and how much I want." Healthy eating and moderation with food is the soundest policy. Also, be careful to regard coffee and other caffeine sources as the right way to fuel up before, during, or after a run. The boost may work initially, but the chances of dehydration and needing a restroom increase.

⚠ Watch out for the twist. Whenever my daughter runs on grass for even a short distance, it's an ankle sprain in waiting. If an alternative exists, avoid spongy surfaces even if it appears harmless. Travel on firm, level surfaces as much as you can because the "shortcut" may lead to an avoidable injury.

⚠ Never forget you will not win against a car. **Trusting an automobile driver, especially at a stoplight or stop sign**, is a middle finger episode waiting to happen, if not worse. On the streets, make sure you have room to veer off safely. Moving towards traffic is advantageous to have less worry about autos sneaking up from behind.

⚠ Heart attacks are no fun. I am just kidding because that is not something to joke about, but the sudden shock of a close-by vehicle puts it in play. For blocked-view alleyways, move far away from the buildings as possible. Staying far from the alley exit will give you an extra second of warning.

⚠ Bikes, yikes! On shared trails, stay clear and check behind you before making any turns to avoid a yelling match. It helps to recognize bicycle riders are as dedicated to their workout as you are.

⚠ Unfortunately, predators are out there. Never become so immersed you are unaware of noise in isolated or dark areas. Of course, the best advice is to avoid remote and uninhabited spots. If in a new location with few people around, give the headphones a break and focus on the surroundings. Even for those fleet-of-foot and self-defense experts, there may be a danger.

70

⚠ **Never, ever, text and run; it can wait**! It's a possible face plant and broken phone in not waiting.

⚠ Remember to display good manners. Give notice to people you approach from behind because one never knows how people may react to the unseen. Stomp on approach or say a quick "Excuse me" or "On left or right." As if driving, cruise on the right, and pass on the left. Even on less-traveled paths, stay to the side for potential passers-by.

Give and return friendly gestures to and from fellow runners. **Acknowledge them because a "brothers and sisters in arms" bond exists**. A slight head nod serves the purpose when lacking the energy for a smile or wave. It also inspires others to know you are proud and happy to be active.

⚠ Watch out for the fork in the road. On unknown streets, neighborhoods, and trails, pay attention. You won't believe how easy it is to get disoriented after a few twists, turns, and miles. Bear in mind that GPS is not always reliable for finding a way out around tall buildings and some locations.

⚠ Slip and slides are not always fun. Never take wet surfaces for granted. Even a slight turn on slick pavement can result in a crash landing.

⚠ Pulled hamstrings are super annoying. Downhill slopes may seem stimulating, but it's easy to get going too fast and out of control. Speed and subsequent slowing can lead to a muscle pull or wipe-out.

⚠ Animals may not be cuddly. **Never trust an animal on the loose or a leash**. Fast movers can threaten animals, so stay clear the best you can. Dog walkers are not happy either after their dog jerks them when you get too close. I have come across a wide variety of other animals, also. Deer, wild turkeys, birds, wild dogs, horses, raccoons, rats, foxes, possums, and coyotes are out there. How does one spell Tetanus?

⚠ The hills are alive; make sure you are up to it, though. Inclines help build leg power and stamina, but they can present danger. I mostly avoid beginning with a climb because the immediate body and heart stress feel dangerous. You should check out your marathon to know the number of slopes and train accordingly. A secret that helps on a steep incline is only looking straight to the ground in front of you. The earth will appear flat instead of the reality of the slope.

Know of Hidden Perils

I'm sure you will discover other road rules on your adventures. I saved the next three for greater emphasis.

⚠ Cheaters never prosper. **Superheroes only exist in the movies, and slackers rarely thrive, so avoid both by following the training schedule.** Doing more than what's called for leads to overuse injuries, and skipping miles lead to being unprepared for the extensive runs.

⚠ Take care of the necessities. Before heading out, calculate your facility stops because little is more critical than needing to relieve oneself. It is a particular issue of old age because this bodily function comes more frequently and out of nowhere. Sober embarrassment may only be a block or two away, so do not leave home before emptying the bladder and again.

Also, depending on where you run the longer distances, it pays to have a few bucks with you. For the grocery mart, drug store, gas station, or fast-food establishment, you may have to buy something to use the restroom. Restroom options are most urgent in the wintertime because trail and park facilities are often closed. If no bathrooms are available, run a path that leads back to your house after so many miles. **Nowadays, someone is always watching, and you do not want to be a viral sensation for a visible act of relief.**

⚠ Social distance is the law of the day. The pandemic necessitates keeping a fair amount away from everyone until further notice. Staying ten feet ahead of other runners is a good plan, of course. Many feet behind are not as cool because someone is beating you, I tease. You may want to avoid public restrooms and watering devices when you can. Take your water bottle, face mask, and hand sanitizer to help with that. The current conditions present new ordeals, but not unmanageable ones.

Now that I've scared you with the possible dangers, don't be alarmed. Nothing is healthier for mental and physical health than getting outside and moving. In time, all the above suggestions become second nature.

A Marathon Legend Capsule

Strong

After discussing the possible running safety measures, this tragic event is unfathomable but indicative of our world, I suppose.

How do you win a marathon without training for it or taking one step in the race? Well, here is how. First, I would never slight the winners of a marathon, especially of the most prestigious of all, the Boston Marathon, but unfortunately, they were an afterthought in 2013.

As this book has been at the intersection of baseball and Marathon running, I include an athlete, a future Hall of Fame baseball player, who I would guess would not even entertain the thought of running 26.2 miles. The 2013 Boston Marathon is forever etched into America's memories whether one knows or cares anything about Marathon running. It was a horrible day, with a bomb exploding, injuring, and killing runners and fans.

Few people remember who won the race that day, but about everyone remembers Baseball Player David Ortiz, who goes by the nickname, Big Papi. With memorable words, David was the winner as he proclaimed a champion's heart a few days later before a Boston Red Sox game, "This is our f - - - ing city and nobody gonna dictate our freedom. Stay Strong." So powerful and appropriate for the occasion, as he displayed what a champion does when they are down – they fight and do not let others dictate the outcome. Big Papi helped restore the city and nation's spirit and made me proud to have been a Major League Player.

I was not in Boston and only observed from afar like most people. But I feel connected to those times when I was about to run the 2017 Las Vegas marathon four years later. The race was only six weeks after the Las Vegas deadly shooting, where so many lost their lives. It was such an eerie feeling to pass by the site of the tragic events, along with having everything go silent for an early stretch of the race. It is one of the times in life when sports seem so inconsequential, yet it is crucial to keep going and observe Big Papi's advice of not letting anyone dictate our freedom.

When searching for the strength to persevere sometimes, I think of the powerful words "Boston Strong" and "Vegas Strong," and I add "Perconte Strong." Yes, when we add "Strong" to anything, it becomes synonymous with the strength to overcome, so it is a good thing to repeat when you feel a lack of energy.

The winners of the 2013 Boston Marathon were Lelisa Desisa Benti and Bizunesh Deba, who replaced a later-disqualified runner. Luckily, the leaders finished before tragedy struck.

My Story: Road Tripping

Understand what we don't know

This might pass This might last

This may grow

Easy come and easy go

Easy left me a long time ago

I'm in the fire but I'm still cold

Nothing works, works for me anymore

To and fro the pendulum throws

Pearl Jam *"Pendulum"*

Jacks Are Lucky

Of the running questions I get, the most frequent one is, "What about your knees?" Yes, the amount of pounding the body's lower half takes is enormous. I can only surmise my years of coaching have kept them durable. I believe throwing batting practice for too many hours to imagine and bending to pick up balls kept my legs strong, and the continuous activity has been the means to my health – as I knock on wood.

I was lucky for the most part in professional baseball, too. I had a few broken noses, a busted knee, a few pulled muscles, and an ankle stress fracture. Over a twelve-year professional run, that is a good record compared to many. But one of my biggest career regrets was not doing what it took to be physically stronger. It is some consolation that the sport was behind with conditioning, and the benefits of strength training and excellent nutrition were a few years away. But I still wish I would have made a more concerted effort to lift weights and eat better. Bigger, stronger, faster, a trite phrase, does apply to reaching athletic potential, so I realize the value of cross-training for distance running.

At one point or another in my second sporting life, I have familiarity with each of the above safety stipulations. It helps to review them regularly, as I do, to have the best chance at remaining healthy.

Fortunately, none have prevented me from training or the marathon. The lessons are clear, though — always pay attention to the surroundings. You never know what may confront you. One time, I encountered a situation I had never imagined, Wild Turkeys! Whoa! My first thought was of Thanksgiving, but the turkeys were looking at me with what seemed to be "Revenge." I gingerly sidestepped my way around them without ever taking my eyes away. I did say "Wild," right? As I said, you never know!

A Trip Well-traveled

All athletes have accidents along the way at some point. The following "trips" have come my way. After each one, I shake my head in disbelief at how fast they occurred.

It is a joyous scene when an athlete kisses the ground. They show gratitude for their art and achievement, but that was not my intent here. Out of nowhere, a seam in the sidewalk jumps. Bang! My toe drills it. The athlete in me expects to gain control in any circumstance, but the fall is unavoidable. It is "self and phone preservation time!" Kissing the ground in this instance was not joyous or in gratitude.

I have come so close to facial injuries each time. Luckily, I got my hands out front and gave the sidewalk a little peck. A few knee, hand, hip cuts, and bruises have been the extent of the damage, but ego damage from the embarrassment remained far longer. In the end, some joy and thankfulness emanate because it could have been much worse.

Maybe the best news was that my phone survived each fall without a scratch. One must have priorities, and after protecting the face, saving one's phone is next on the list. A few scrapes to the knees and hands won't feel as bad as dealing with a destroyed cell phone. I am only half-joking. The secret is to release your phone forward as you are about to hit the ground. For phones in the pocket, your last thought is, "Why didn't I invest in an armband phone holder?" Such is life in the fast lane.

Of course, I've used the cellphone armband holder before and still found a way to slip on a turn and destroy the phone. I do not know of any foolproof phone safety devices, so I prefer to hold my phone in my hand so I have some control over it.

The by-product of a few scrapes is a minor price to pay, and it takes more than a small crack to disrupt an athlete. In summary, to maintain health, keep your eyes and ears wide open, knees up, fuel up, and play smart.

6
The Beginner's Mindset

A Dream

I am on an out-of-control, never-ending rollercoaster, and my emotional state is the same.

I wake and deliberate what it means? The explanation is simple — marathon training has begun. For those who are big fans of roller coasters, training will be right up your alley. I am more the plodding trolley type guy. I prefer to check out the surroundings casually, but my career prepared me for both experiences.

"It is nothing more than a series of arguments between the part of your brain that wants to stop and the part that wants to keep going."

Definition of a marathon by an unknown author

More real words never were than the quote above, and runners who travel far know that reality.

The success trail involves sweat; there is no way around it or the associated lessons.

Stairway to success:

11. Hard work

12. In the moment

13. Attitude

14. Dodging over-confidence

15. Nature of sports performance

16. Recovery

1st Month Training Steps – Miles 1 - 8

Heed the Lessons of Sports

You will find out the marathon and training are mental roller coasters. One week or mile feels like an uphill struggle, followed by a carefree downhill excursion. The anticipation of the end and the surety "you got this" precedes high uncertainty. It's a series of up and down, even though most movement entails endless miles on flat ground.

First, congratulate yourself before week one for completing the many preparation details, knowing the work begins with your goal, purpose, plan, health rules, and habits set. It's time to find out what you got and what being a competitor is all about. **The lessons of sports will come fast and furious now.** Please pay attention to them, so you will be ready to apply the knowledge when it counts most in the marathon. **Learning from practice is** fundamental for getting the conclusion you want while failing to capture and use the experience will haunt the athlete in the heat of competition.

Step eleven – putting in the work. Winners prepare to give more than ever before and know **that no shortcuts exist**. Not even the superstars can go out and just do it. Every sport requires a work ethic that leads to development, and running is no exception. One must go from mile one to two to create the physicality to keep moving up the mile ladder. Suffice it to say, adhering to the daily schedule, and the weekly mileage amount is the basis of training. **Trust in the workout timetable is prime, knowing there is a method to the madness.**

Step twelve — staying in the moment. Productive athletes manage their time well by not **dwelling on mistakes or jumping to conclusions**. They deal with the "Now," have a short memory, and forgive themselves for the inevitable errors. Those who have difficulty getting over blunders become unhappy and often quit.

A key to marathon training is not to brood over the entire schedule because it can seem overwhelming with the many miles and weeks to go. When I catch myself worrying about how I can finish 13 after being sluggish and depleted from five miles, I refer to my playing days again. I know the importance of playing them one game at a time and "grinding each day out."

I've learned to **keep this perspective — I only have to do today's run, so it does no good to worry about tomorrow.** I've also found a lousy day doesn't have to lead to more of them.

Maintain Perspective — Early Training Miles

Once the five-mile range doesn't seem so hard, you are in a comfortable spot. Most training schedules have you travel up to that amount for most of the weekly runs. The first month's longest run will get you to about the eight-mile mark. A good tip is not to arrange much activity afterward on the long run day because you will want to "chill" after. For that reason, scheduling your extended treks on a non-workday is beneficial.

Step thirteen — cultivating an attitude of optimism and excitement. Before a game, the athlete's approach is critical, and looking at it as if it's a hopeful opportunity creates eagerness and energy. To help your running mood, upon waking, do not say, 'I have to run x number of miles today." **The "have to's" defeat the purpose, so instead substitute "I get to."** Another way to add enthusiasm is to **have a physical destination** for the longer runs. For example, it's daunting to think of 14 miles, but traveling to Navy Pier and back, 14 miles in total, excites me. A physical destination gives more motivation than a mileage amount, which may depress.

Step fourteen — avoiding over-confidence. Some runners may put the early training miles on cruise control. A cakewalk beginning may cause you to run faster or do more miles than scheduled, but that result is fool's gold because it can lead to injury and burnout. Just wait! The first few weeks and miles are the start of a long road ahead. A good reminder is the unfulfilled New Year's resolutions to get in shape, only to quit the proposal soon. From the start, work on finding a comfortable pace and sticking with the schedule, period.

Step fifteen — knowing sports are unpredictable. This phase is a natural follow-up lesson **and one you probably already know.** Like the beginning of any life mission, what follows is an unknown. The first day of school or work does not go the way you anticipated. You know no one and worry about acceptance, and everybody is friendly and accommodating. Conversely, you go with high expectations, and the culture gives off unexpected vibes. With life and sports — you never know with each time out a variable.

Sometimes you expect to feel great, and it's a struggle from the start. On other occasions, you have no thrill in going that day, but the body and mind rise and compete well. Or you may start sluggish, and after several miles, you come around. And the opposite, you feel unbeatable initially, and it turns into drudgery. **Bear in mind the highs and lows are the nature and mystery of competition.** One can only hope there are more good days than bad.

Know the Value in Recovery

Step sixteen — bouncing back after rough outings. Perhaps nothing defines you as an athlete more than this. Even the top players have off days, but their ability to perform up to standards after a slump keeps them ready for the next game. The running schedule's constancy makes the ups and downs inevitable, demanding mental and physical recovery.

Physical Mending

Inescapably, you will have soreness and even hard-to-get-over pain. For some, walking itself may be a chore after extended runs. The saving grace is soreness is a sign you extended beyond past efforts, so it's no time to give up. **Embrace the challenge of bouncing back, knowing you will be better off the next time.** Stretching exercises, a cold shower, Epsom salts bath, and a roller stick are helpful. As a last resort, muscle pain relievers are invaluable when the other options fail. You will also want to be sure to drink and eat soon after runs.

Mental Healing

The thing is, the body soreness will go away. The psychological test may be harder to overcome. As indicated before, bouncing back is about **forgetting the unproductive games and looking to the next one as a new opportunity**. The optimistic frame of mind is the way to go with a deep-seated belief it will work out for the best, no matter how discouraged.

If nothing else, pro baseball taught me the necessity of rising after failure. First, the nature of hitting at that level is success three out of ten at-bats. I had many dry spells that lasted many games and at-bats, which added to the pressure to produce. Second, many disappointments came from remaining at the same level, along with many demotions and releases. I learned to roll with the punches and expect better the next day.

It's vital to understand confidence will come and go in sports, and those who can regain it have the highest chance to persevere. The key is never to stop believing you can turn things around no matter how poorly things are in the present. I do my best to **nurture the mental side, build the ego, and prepare for the next run with self-talk motivational phrases.**

Here are ones I have drafted and often use:

- "I am an accomplished runner and athlete. I willfully choose to do this."

- "No amount of tiredness and soreness will deter my focus from my intent."

- Nothing feels better to an athlete than "Rising to the occasion."

- "I got this, and I'm not going to let others, my mind, or body tell me I don't."

- "I am one week closer to my dream coming true."

- "Pain is temporary; quitter is not who I am."

- "Giving my all today is all I can do."

- "The willingness to persevere is what sets me apart from others."

  And two of my favorites from others, "Don't *confuse difficulty with failure."* **Eric Orton,** and from the movie, *A League of Their Own,* "The hard is what makes it great."

Takeaways from the First Month

- Recall or learn the lessons of sports to apply in games and life.

- Slacking leads to failure; committing to a daily work ethic is a must.

- Don't get over-confident and do too much too soon.

- It's not about starting fast but about having enough "inside" to stay the course.

- When overwhelmed, repeat to yourself, "I only have to do today."

- Realize what you can control – effort; and what you can't – results.

- Don't jump to conclusions; count on good and bad training days.

- Stay with the schedule, plan, and routine.

- Revel in the sense of accomplishment with each additional mile you go.

Finally, never forget it's what you do after you fail that counts.

A Marathon Legend Capsule

A Man for the Ages

How do you get the inspiration to do something? One way is to look to those who offer it.

"Great is the victory, but the friendship is all the greater."

One has to love someone with the above philosophy, mostly when they were one of the greatest runners of all time, Emil Zatopek. I say that because it's not that some top athletes are just into themselves, but often, "They are just into themselves." I joke but also know there is some truth to it. The Czechoslovakian gregarious long-distance runner had a weird running style, which only means it's not how; it's that one gets it done. He often opined because they didn't grade on the form, he would continue with his awkward gait. "It isn't gymnastics or figure skating, you know," were his exact words. In the 1952 Helsinki Olympic games, Zatopek, on a whim, decided to run the Marathon after having won the five- and ten-thousand-kilometer races. Despite never running one before, Emil won the Marathon in world-breaking time. Emil was innovative with his training techniques, emphasizing the necessity of creativity and adjustments in one's routine.

I'm inclined to call him by his first name here because after reading about him, one feels like they would like him and want to be his friend. Along with being one of the greatest runners of all time, Emil stands out for his generous, outgoing personality. He spoke of the Olympic Games significance after World War 2 here:

"For me, the 1948 Olympics was a liberation of the spirit. After all those dark days of the war, the bombing, the killing, the starvation, the revival of the Olympics was as if the sun had come out. I went into the Olympic Village in 1948, and suddenly there were no more frontiers, no more barriers. Just the people meeting together. It was wonderfully warm. Men and women who had lost five years of life were back again."

Such beautiful words that have extra meaning after the world has been through a global pandemic. Emil left his mark and is a man admired all these years later. Unfortunately, Zatopek's life wasn't all glorious. After voicing his support for democracy, he went against the reigning Communist party, which forced him into hard-labor jobs for years.

Perhaps his enduring legacy is it's better to stand for freedom than run for repression.

My Story: Beginnings are Only That

Look, If you had one shot or one opportunity

To seize everything you ever wanted

One moment

Would you capture it or just let it slip?

Eminem *Lose Yourself"*

Stutter Starts

I know first-hand what it's like to start and do too much too early. On my first day in the major leagues, I am obviously "Jacked," and I proceed to take tons of pre-game groundballs. My energy was off the charts, and I was out to impress my new coaches. The result was heavy legs for a few days after. My first major league at-bat, which came a couple of days later, was against sound judgment, too. I hardly ever swung at the first pitch as it was not my nature. Instead of sticking with my routine, I offered at the first pitch, which resulted in an easy out. Both instances were lessons learned – temper the enthusiasm and stay within yourself.

Beginnings are often baffling. An example I can give you is as a 16-year-old, I had played in a baseball tournament in Murray, Kentucky. I fell in love with the college field there, even though we played on a community field for the tourney. In my senior year of high school, I applied to Murray State University. The good news was I received a modest academic scholarship from the school, so I wrote

89

to the coach about my interest in playing there. The bad news came with a coach's letter saying their best player was an underclass second baseman, my position. He advised that Murray was not a good fit for me as far as playing. I appreciated his honesty, but I attended anyway.

My strengths were good speed, quickness, hand-eye coordination, and a good swing. My drawbacks were a weak arm, lousy throwing mechanics, stiff hands, no power, and a lack of confidence. Fortunately, the positives outweighed the negatives, and I made the team. I had only eight plate appearances during my freshman year. But I got a boost for returning from the coach, saying he would work out more playing time the following year. That was enough to want to return. The rest is history, and the coach, Johnny Reagan, was the most influential person for getting me to pro ball. I discovered beginnings do not always indicate the outcomes, and results can surprise when one does not jump to conclusions.

Another odd start occurred in my first professional experience. I arrived at the Los Angeles Dodgers A-ball team with unreal excitement and first-day unease. Arriving too late to dress for the game, I watched the end of an embarrassing loss by my new team. My unmet, new manager went on a post-game, F-bomb rant that doubled the number I heard the word in the past. How do you say, "Intimidating?" I soon realized the unmentionable, and the rant came with the business. Our irate coach threatened changes to the team, and he proved a man of his word. Naivety went out the door that day, and his lecture was a wake-up call.

Once again, I learned from the experience. One, people come and go a lot in high-level business. " Two, "Produce or get lost," is how the system works. Pro sports are a "What have you done for me lately" proposition. Even though the start was rocky, the manager proved to be fair and helped further my career. Once again, my past warns me the beginning of marathon training can be a rocky road.

The Nature of Kick-Offs

Beginnings typically have positive prospects and enthusiasm, along with some cautious anticipation. Spring Training began each year with painful reflections from the previous season behind me. I expect to make the team and have the best year of my career, but I know not to get overconfident. It may seem easy at the start but changes quickly. It never took long to say, "I forgot how good major league pitching is," and "It is harder to stand out than expected." I try my best to trust I am good enough to hang with the world's finest players, but many sleepless nights follow.

The season itself is a long haul with many uncertainties. I got off to a promising start many seasons, only to have hiccups along the way. Early success led to a false sense of security, while some slow starts led to some solid years. A slump can be an effective motivator because it forces the player to attend to the basics.

The same sense comes with marathon training. With experience on my side and the body feeling strong, I am ready and optimistic things will be easier. However, anxiety shows up soon with the inquiry, "Why do I feel this bad with no apparent improvement?" It all goes back to sports' nature – past results are not predictive of future ones. Even though familiarity helps with the obstacles, each year of training is hard work. A mile stays the same each year, no matter how many times one has done it.

The education I found from beginnings are threefold:

· The ride's uneventful part only lasts a short while before trouble arrives.

· The mental game one employs to handle the rollercoaster of emotions is the difference-maker.

· Small wins along the path are the avenue to the World Series and the finish line.

7

The Identity Mindset

Living a Dream

In my earlier life, I wasn't Jack Perconte, but Jack Perconte, "The ballplayer." Often, I would hear this from acquaintances, "Oh, you're the ballplayer."

When you dedicate yourself to a goal, it has a way of becoming who you are.

"There will be days you don't think you can run a marathon. There will be a lifetime of knowing you have."
The Runner's High

Winning is all about going from doubt to the sweet smell of success.

The success trail keeps winding and challenging. Maintaining a sense of self is crucial.

Stairway to success:

17. Identity

Step into Being a Runner

Step 17 — embracing the identity you have created for yourself. Once people seem to add a description to you, you have made it, in a sense. No longer will you be You, but John/Jane Doe, the Runner. The new identity feels good because it identifies you as a person with extraordinary discipline. The self and others' recognition of that pushes you to live up to it. It not only feels good to have an identity, and it associates you with an activity for a long time, if not forever.

Jokes about marathon runners are abundant, and you may have some of your own. These two favorites of mine are undeniably accurate. "How do you know someone has run a marathon? Wait a few minutes, and they will let you know." "The most difficult part of running a marathon is working it into every conversation for the next year." Or for the rest of your life, I might add. For those who run far, we sense an obligation to tell others.

Once again, I am guilty of the above, but I have sound reasons for the boasting. Sure, I am proud of the achievement, but mostly, the more people who know, the more I'm indebted to finishing the task. Involving others motivates me not to want to let anyone down by not finishing the race. Friends and acquaintance's queries of how things are going push you to work harder. It would be painful to answer, "I didn't finish." That's my reasoning, and I'm sticking to it, and thus this book.

Here's the thing, if you never get to a finish line, being a runner is worth it. The benefits of more miles than you have ever run, less stress, and fewer pounds on the scale are merely the beginning. The "runner" identity helps your life outlook and something to claim as your own. Handily, you have a ready answer when people ask you to tell them about yourself. "I'm a Runner" is a good conversation starter, and upon meeting a fellow runner or athlete, you can talk for hours and form a relationship.

Following are the occurrences that make you a Runner's Club member, and I'm sure you can add some items to this list. For those scoring at home, you enjoy running if you do a few of them. If you do more than a few, it's love. Doing most means you are an addict, like me, and like most addictions, you may annoy others occasionally, which is another thing that goes with the territory.

You know you love to run when:

1. The first and last considerations you have each day are what time you will run that day or the next.

2. Your philosophy after eating an extra piece of pizza, cake, or anything is planning an extra mile or two the next workout.

3. You take pride in displaying discipline, and it shows in all areas of your life.

4. Water is your "go-to" drink. And you never go long without having it by your side. It provides an opening to talk about your running life with the waiter, friends, and acquaintances.

5. Whenever a family member asks what you need for a gift occasion, it's always "Running Shoes." After a while,

they stop asking, and you have pairs in reserve, which is a comforting sentiment.

6. Even nasty Porta Potties can seem like heaven when you "Gotta" go.

7. You have "peace of mind" after a long, effortless run, knowing those come only occasionally.

8. You know exercise is a must for a perfect day.

9. You are proficient at using the "My Trip" car mileage gauge. It's a priority to find, calculate, and verify distances. I am showing my age with this one as I'm sure the younger generation can pull up lengths on their phone" app."

10. An essential practice at the week's beginning is studying the weather forecast for the upcoming one. Devising the schedule is of utmost importance because you do not want to get stuck having to run at awkward times. You become an expert at finding a window on suspect weather days and analyzing the radar. Preparing for "ugly" conditions is challenging when no opening exists, but you always figure something out.

You know you are a running addict when:

11. Before an out-of-town trip, you check out the area to see if it has running paths within proximity to where you stay. Of course, almost anywhere, except the middle of the ocean, is a workable space for a dedicated runner.

12. If you go more than two days in a row without jogging, you start bouncing off the walls.

13. You measure the quality of a run by how many times you asked yourself, "WTF, why am I putting myself through this?" Any number of times higher than ten means total loser for that day.

14. When another runner goes flying by, chest out, you whisper, "Hey Champ, I will be out here long after you drop." You know the tortoise eventually catches and passes the hare! When you see them stop or turn around before you, you whisper, "You Wimp; I'm just warming up."

15. You check your watch or running application a lot to stay on pace or make it look that way. For me, it's to make sure I am going slow enough, with the knowledge that "speed kills" at this stage of my life, anyway.

16. You chuckle when people suggest it's too hot or cold to run outside.

17. You love having family and friends over to hang out and equally fancy when they do not overstay so you can get to your day's workout.

18. You wear your marathon finisher shirt everywhere, and maybe even to a church service.

19. You can share experiences with other serious runners for hours, even if you are an introvert.

20. You pay attention to any marathon news, specifically reports on the big races, and know the time of year they

are. When the Olympics come around, you are one of the few that look forward to and watch the marathon races.

21. You have running nightmares and beautiful dreams of winning the Boston Marathon. Yes!

Signs you are just plain "Sick" when it comes to running

22. When anyone asks how far a landmark is from the house, you can give them the exact distance to the tenth of a mile. From my location in Chicago, the Drake hotel is 5.75 miles away. Navy Pier is 7.1 miles to the rear of the attraction. Wrigley Field is 3062.5 strides. I am kidding on that last one, but I may be close to correct.

23. You find a way of slipping out on fully booked days and always have run clothes and shoes handy no matter where you are. You are super proficient at the two-minute shower and dressing fast.

24. You can put the time in slow motion. Yes, after a long run, and your body is in a satisfied state of calm, life seems to slow down. It's a hard sensation to describe, but time, attention, and movements move at a sloth's pace. If you propose to do something in ten minutes, it will take thirty minutes. The idea of even standing is repugnant with such comfort.

25. You answer with "Just" or "Only" before the distance after someone asks how far you are going that day. "Yea, but just 10 miles." Listeners judge you are bragging. It may come off that way, but you honestly mean it. After all, ten is minor compared to the 26.2 miles and many

distances one must cover in training. For close friends, you may feel cocky and respond with, "Til I win." "Until the ground cries, Uncle," "Until the treadmill tires." Even though the cockiness feels good, be careful because the next run may be a real bear or bore.

26. You have difficulty getting rid of worn-out exercise clothing and shoes because you believe you will need them at some point. Until a shirt looks dreadful or shoes with many holes, you keep them. It's fighting terms if a family member suggests throwing away an old, hard-earned marathon shirt. Exercise clothes fill my drawers, and shoes are everywhere in my house, old and new, each with a purpose and for all-weather occasions.

27. You find it hard to walk around your neighborhood out of fear of destroying your identity as the Guy/Gal constantly on the move. It hurts to imagine my neighbors might think I have lost energy or a step or two. It pays to have a dog to walk, so you keep your image if you must stroll!

28. People stop asking what you are doing today, tomorrow, or this week because the answer is always, "I'm running." People close to you occasionally question your life priorities because you seem to put exercise before relationships. Sometimes, the query is necessary, I might add.

29. Running is your solution for about everything. For example, I run to get rid of the following conditions.

* Stress

* Headache

* Body pain

* Upset stomach

* Overeating

* Insomnia

* Writer's block

* Annoying people

* Lethargy

Please consider, though; I am not a doctor, just my way of looking at exercise. Once pain is intense and unending, seek medical advice.

30. You get offended and correct people when they mention a marathon is 26 miles, leaving out the .2

31. Often, you choose the stairs option instead of the elevator.

32. Your pedometer stopping is the same as being "unfriended" by your best buddy.

33. And when you see runners go by, you think out of jealousy, "That should be me," especially on a gorgeous day.

34. You analyze each runner's form and decide if they have or could run a marathon. Joggers who have no rhythm or bounce to their movement equals no chance.

35. Even on Holidays, you find time to get your workout in, and family members get to the point of expecting it of you. It's most necessary at Christmas because most of your gifts have to do with fitness, anyway.

36. You are back on the trails two days after a marathon.

I draw the line at putting a "26.2" decal on my car, but to each his own. It's an impressive feat, so it's OK to wear it if you want.

A Marathon Legend Capsule

A "Long" Road

Talk about running being in one's soul.

Every once in a while, you come across a story that seems so incredible you can only shake your head in amazement. After typing "Matt Long runner" into an internet search, many inspirational articles about him result. For a long story short, no pun intended, Matt Long survived a horrific accident in which most people would not have survived, let alone recover.

Having run a marathon before the accident in a fabulous time of three hours and thirteen minutes, Matt overcame catastrophic injuries to run another. As I have written continually here, the physical accomplishment is one thing and tremendously formidable in his case. But until he could wrap his mind around the situation, recovery, and the thought of ever running again, let alone a marathon, was the difference-maker. First, Matt states, "I wanted to be an athlete again, and I wanted to be myself again." I cannot say it's the same because I have never experienced anything close to him, but I relate to the part of wanting to remain an athlete and embracing the identity one sets for themself.

The second thing he says that speaks to the heart of accomplishment is, "Then I decided to change my attitude from I want to do something to I will do something. And that made the difference." I agree with Matt because it's the attitude one brings to the plate that determines the outcome, or at least a chance for a favorable one. The achievers deal in thoughts about the possible, not the opposite of that.

His story also backs up something I wrote earlier here of everyone finding their purpose in life, which is different for all. Matt understandably lost his for a spell after the accident but came to realize the necessity to inspire others with his life story. He has done that task well.

In his book, *The Long Road*, Matt Long shares his unbelievable comeback story, and if a movie isn't in the works, I would be surprised.

My Story: Earning My Running Stripes

Yeah, I'm running down a dream

That never would come to me

Working on a mystery, going wherever it leads

I'm runnin' down a dream

Tom Petty *"Running Down a Dream"*

Expectation

The major leagues proved to be a battle I never conquered, in my estimation, because I never felt I belonged at the highest level. I believed I earned the top promotion, but once there, it proved difficult to see myself as a "Big Leaguer." Without confidence, the daily mental battle was exhausting. Thus, it wasn't easy to enjoy my career as one would expect. I also came to realize, just making it to the big leagues wasn't enough. The thing is, I needed a measure of success to have satisfaction. Fortunately, after a horrible start, enough came for some lifelong contentment. I've relished in the big-leaguer identity, and it's an accomplishment no one can take away. The same outlook applies to being a runner. I enjoy being one, but I need to finish each marathon training and race, and anything less is losing.

Graduation Days

I can't say when I earned the label "A Runner." I guess a good indicator was not being able to go more than a few days without lacing up the shoes and upon entering my first marathon.

But as indicated, I wanted more defining moments to earn the designation. One such moment occurred in my first marathon. I had done the training and prepared the right way to have a solid run but developed a calf cramp in mile nine. Of course, my first words are, "No way this can be happening. I train hard for five months, and after only nine miles – WTH?" I had a decision to make. Should I stop because the pre-race advice was, "If you get injured, stop because it most likely will lead to a more sizable one?" My answer came from the athlete in me, "No way am I stopping."

I relied on my professional athlete background and played with the pain. I developed a sense of the difference between hurt and injured, so I file the cramp under the first category. I kept moving and hoping. It worked, and miraculously, the pang went away at mile 16 after hobbling and walking for 7 miles. I must be a runner after that!

I earned my stripes in another marathon when my iPod played four songs before stopping for the day. It's another "You have got to be joking" moment. No one informed the instrument precisely what a marathon is — not 2.6 miles but 26.2 miles. Music inspires me and helps divert the mind from the constant loping, so to run almost the entire way without song proved I was a runner.

Instances keep happening, which confirms my runner status. One year, I had foot soreness near my big toe for five months of training. No matter how far I ran, some pain existed, and I walked tenderly after long runs. It was never so painful I could not keep going, but ice and Ibuprofen were a post-run necessity. I knew race day *would create a test of my ability to withstand the ache and find out if I needed to see a foot specialist. Well, not a day since finishing the 26.2 miles has there been a pain in that foot. The marathon cured the issue. I question, "How the heck does that happen?" but I am not complaining, and it's a fascination that brings gratitude. But I repeat, I am not a doctor, even though I connect the dots and view exercise as a semi-miracle cure-all.*

Finally, I've validated being a runner with a self-given nickname. You know you are "Bigtime" when you have an alter ego. Inspired by the names in the book, Born to Run, I am now "Sussurratore di Corso" when running. The nickname is Italian for the Running Whisperer. It seemed appropriate, at least to me. Other handles considered were The Plodding Turtle, The Writing Nag, The Trudging Tramp, and the Shuffling Snail. They describe my pace, but the Running Whisperer is most appropriate because of my writing, Italian heritage, and plan to get much faster in the future, I jest. If you spot me out on the trail, you can call me "Suss" or "Suss di" because of the lengthy full nickname. Thank You. Finally, I recommend all runners give themselves a handle, even if they never tell anyone 0f it.

8

The Athlete's Mindset

A Dream

I'm sailing along and smiling because it's one of my most enjoyable runs ever. Then, wouldn't you know it, the ground begins to shake, and an earthquake erupts. Then, I twist my ankle on an unseen hole, but I am too scared to stop, so I keep going. Next, I cannot avoid a giant opening and fall into a large hole, and I am lying among a million snakes. I climb out and keep going. Many runners are behind me now, but they appear dead and are chasing me. What else can go wrong? My only thought is to do what it takes to get back home.

Wow, I'm happy to wake from the most common nightmares all in one long night. The message of it is clear to me — adversity comes to all athletes, and it's rare to have an uncomplicated trip.

"One run can change your day, and many runs can change your life." **Author Unknown**

Any worthwhile destination begins with baby steps, followed by a few more.

The success trail delves deeper into the mind the further one goes. The mental game is often the governing factor to the end.

Stairway to success:

18. Brain power

19. Overcoming with hopefulness

2nd Month Training Steps – Miles 9 – 13.1

Become a First-Rate Athlete

At this stage of training, you have achieved runner status by consistently doing it and going beyond the ordinary. Now on the trek to the half marathon, **it elevates you to a whole other level – you are no doubt a prime athlete.**

What sets you apart is you undoubtedly have had to overcome some severe trials to get this far, so the willingness to keep going separates you from the quitters. The hunger for the competition and future tests puts one in the elevated athlete status because scampering 13.1 miles requires an enviable spirit of determination and commitment. Many similar traits apply here — grit, persistence, perseverance, resolve, purpose, and willpower. **In the simplest terms, stick-to-itiveness is the means of completing the mission.**

Rise Higher

So, how do you attain the intensity level to do more than before? First, athletes must learn not to take any opponent lightly, which in this instance is the pronounced number of miles and your inner being. Some activities get more comfortable the more you do it, but running a long way is not one of those. If you go out with a carefree approach, the miles seem unending, and finishing the day's run may not happen. **You must give extra attention and practice to the large runs.**

Step eighteen — recognizing the brain can do the extraordinary and is the ultimate difference-maker. The critical point is the body will only respond to what the mind tells it. You will find your mental game determines what you can do each workout, and the initial key to a start is getting "psyched up." And although getting pumped may not solve all the anguish, it is crucial for persevering through the harshest tests. **If you do not adjust your thinking for the extended mileage, you ask for a struggle, if not defeat.**

Prepare for "Special"

Another advantage from my past was my experience with opening days, playoffs, and championship games. The occasions came with added excitement and pressure, and I figured out how to prepare for them more than regular-season games. The marathon training schedule includes a much longer run one day a week, and **one must treat those as playoff games, with the World Series, the marathon, to come later**.

The following are some suggestions for rising to the big events:

❖ Remind yourself the big occasions are the daring adventures athletes crave.

❖ Target the large-run day early in the week as a special one.

❖ Prepare for it as a long-awaited family gathering or as if it will be on TV.

❖ A few days before, visualize the action and the physical destination point. Convince yourself you cannot wait to be on the route and see the destined spot.

❖ Include friends and family with how excited you are for the elite test.

❖ The night before, gather the things you need and prepare everything to make the next day seem different and less troublesome.

❖ Plan premium listening subjects. One trick I use is not listening to my favorite music for a long time leading up to the extended runs. Another worthwhile plan is having an enormous playlist of favorites, so the tunes come infrequently. Both moves have me looking forward to the outings because the songs are fresh again.

❖ Eat, drink, and rest the night before in a manner that sets it apart from the ordinary. Of course, when I say drink, I am not talking of alcoholic beverages.

❖ Wake with eagerness and energy because the day you've been waiting for is here, at last.

⁝ Before heading out the door, read about a person (athlete) you admire and check out some creative quotes to have for reflection.

Preparing for the big days brings memories of your sports past, thrilling itself. As implied, no guarantee comes that gearing up will make the run doable, either, but it gives you hope, and **hope is all an athlete can expect, sometimes.** Upon finishing, revel in the achievement as if you were the star performer, no matter how big a struggle it was. **You came, you played, you conquered – it is what makes you who you are – a runner and an athlete!**

Have Answers for Insecurity

The thing about challenging endeavors is the dreaded self-doubt comes for all, no matter how confident one may be. For the long treks, the reality of what you got yourself into sets forth as well as the fact it is never a cakewalk. After ten or so miles, you are at the stage when a mile can seem twice the earlier ones. Inevitably, self-doubt shows with queries like, "Are you kidding me, only one mile since the last one?" "Seriously, for the marathon, I have to go another 13 miles after a half-marathon?" And "How in the world am I ever going to get more out of myself; I've given all I have?" Of course, I left out the expletives, which are a natural part of those inquiries, too. Also, note that uncertainty crops up at the beginning of training a lot, too, as the body is just rounding into shape. The early weeks are probably the ones I say this the most, "There is no way I will ever make the marathon distance." And that statement comes even after having completed the race many times before.

Step nineteen — handling adversity and skepticism in a way that keeps one optimistic. Know this — those who turn to a negative frame of mind will have trouble proceeding. The remedy for finishing is productively dealing with hardship and doubt. A start to that is to elicit the occasions you had to dig deep in life. A sport's background helps, but any challenging period in one's life provides a guide and motivation. Recall any endeavor that required dedication and perseverance to help you overcome obstacles. Maybe it was to pass a test, talk to a troubled friend, deal with personal depression, or make the team. Anything that took an actual gut check to get through is worth analyzing. **Then, withdraw the strategies used to get through the period and apply them to persevere.** It is helpful to write your tactics so that you can refer to them later, too.

Another way to overcome distress is to consider the identity you have created. **Once you can run a half-marathon, feel free to consider yourself a professional athlete.** It may not be the true definition of a pro because you are not getting paid, but you are one because of the consistent training. For proof, you are elite, ask a professional player if they would shadow you on your next ten-mile run. A laugh is a likely result, knowing they could not stay with you, or at the least, have the desire to. **The better you are at convincing yourself you are extraordinary, the easier it will be to keep moving in severe stages, and upholding the image of you as an athlete to others is an impetus, too.**

Another lesson for the competitor is not to expect their A-game every time. The body is reliable on many runs, but the mind is not, or it's the opposite scenario. Again, it's valuable to recall previous lessons of having a short memory and sport's nature. After failure, one must learn from it and let it go from memory. It's over, but with the tenacity to keep at it, good things follow. **It's also worth never forgetting another sentiment from earlier — worthwhile things do not come easy.**

For some, getting to the half marathon may be elusive at first. Not only will skepticism arrive, but some pain has probably crept into your body. But once you progress to above ten miles, hold your head high because you are in a small percentage of people who have done it. You are a superior athlete, even if you run not one step further.

Takeaways from the Second Month

* Getting "pumped up" for the big contests gives a clear avenue to not being an "also-ran."

* Certainty leads to skepticism quickly in sports. You will sense you have it made one minute, but something pops up to kill the notion.

* At the end of the day, not letting weariness and pain win is the solution to ultimate success.

* A short memory is vital, so do not let failed attempts get the best of you. Of all the sport's lessons, believing tomorrow is a new day is a crucial one.

* The athlete's unshakable commitment to doing their utmost is the appropriate defense to self-doubt.

A Marathon Legend Capsule

It's a Small World Afterall

This runner had to live with thoughts of staying alive and went on to be one of the best. I would say that is overcoming adversity.

In 1980 and 1981, I was a teammate on the Los Angeles Dodgers with the great pitcher, Fernando Valenzuela. Although not in the Hall of Fame, his career was remarkable. Fernando was one of 12 children and grew up in a house on a small farm. He did not play organized baseball until his teenage years and became one of his generation's best. To have a movement named after you like "Fernandomania" is legendary stuff.

During those years, a young boy is on the other side of the world, in the country of Eteria. Sometimes, he and his family had to flee their home to escape brutal massacres. He saw sights no person, let alone a child, should ever have to witness. Having to flee their country, his family eventually made it to the United States. That young boy, Meb Keflezighi, became a U.S. citizen and one of the all-time best marathon runners.

He did not see a car until ten years old or a T.V. until eleven. Years later, Meb stated he ran upon seeing cars, thinking they were death machines. He must have thought it ironic him chasing the lead car in the major marathons he won like the Boston and New York Marathons. He also had second and fourth-place finishes in the Olympic games. His running achievements are fantastic, and along with his high character, he was named a recipient of the

114

Outstanding American by Choice award in 2017. Meb Keflezighi believes in giving back as he does with books about running.

It's incredible to think of the obstacles some must jump over to reach unbelievable heights. Stories like Fernando's and Meb's give me a reason to pause when feeling sorry for myself whenever things do not go my way.

My Story: Lessons Learned

Oh, I must stop these doubts, all these worries

If I don't I just know I'll turn back

I must dream of the things I am seeking

I am seeking the courage I lack

The courage to serve them with reliance

The Sound of Music *"I Have Confidence"*

Disappointment Road

The higher one moves up the career ladder, the predictable hardship and pressure elevate disappointment and anxiety levels.

I know a thing or two about that. For example, I get the dreaded tap on the shoulder and message, "The skipper wants to see you in his office." Seeing how it's the last day of spring training, this cannot be good, and it isn't. "Jack, you are like a son to me, but we are sending you down." If I heard those words once, it seemed a thousand times. My view was, "Could you consider me a distant cousin instead and keep me on the team?" Of course, I never said it; the disappointment would set in, and it was off to the minor leagues again. I felt like a loser, even one step from being among the "elites" in the sport.

Unfortunately, the sinking mood was not a bad dream but a reality. I have a sense of despair after wanting something so

116

much, and the thought of, "Is this even worth it anymore?"
followed. But I also understood nothing of this magnitude
would be easy. I realized it was another time in one's life to
get the feet back on the ground and go back to work.
Fortunately, the outcome changed for me in future years.
Yet, I played with many ballplayers who never got the break
to play in the major leagues. However, they were superior
players and winners who didn't catch a break. Luck goes
both ways in sports and life.

Must-knows for Training and Living

The similarities between the baseball season and a
marathon are not surprising. Both involve successful and
confident building days, followed by failure and hesitancy.
Both pastimes give a harsh reminder of the "Thrill of
Victory" and the "Agony of Defeat." I learned in my career
to manage both sensations by maintaining an even keel. For
example, I took things in stride after a fantastic 5-hit MLB
game in Baltimore, followed by a three-strikeout one the
very next day in Yankee Stadium. Often, I had no confidence
and came away with a few hits. And on others, I was sure of
success, only to get the 0-for that game. The quickness that
confidence and good results disappear in sports is mind-
boggling and why an even attitude is critical. Occasionally
though, no matter how steady a demeanor, sleepless nights
and personal anger were unavoidable.

The same attitude comes with running. I coast early, and a
few minutes later, my entire being questions whether I have
anything left. Self-doubt is a constant companion while
competing against the cream of the crop - the 26,2-mile
opponent. I've come to discover every run is a new
adventure, and rebounding after disappointment is evidence

of the fighter one must be. Of all the advice herein, it's crucial to understand finishing a marathon won't happen if you are unwilling to go the extra mile in training. If you give in and walk or stop when times get tough in practice, the same will happen on race day.

A Painful Conundrum

The right choices are rarely evident in the heat of the moment. For example, I wish I would have played through some aches in my career, while other times, I would have benefited from not pushing through them. One season, after taking a fouled ball off the foot, the pain was immense. I should have told the manager I would give the team what I could after a no-broken bone diagnosis. Instead, I said I could not go, which was a big mistake because the correct approach was "If it ain't broke, play."

On the other hand, I played for a while with a splint on my broken finger and proceeded not to play well. My already little confidence went out the door. It was another mistake. In this case, the soundest decision would have been to wait for the break to heal.

The point is it's hard to make the right call — to know when to back off and when to go, which is another nature of the sports beast. Analyzing the past is all one can rely on in the heat of the action. With running, weak spots begin to throb around mile 10 for me. The initial problem is either the right-side lower back or right lower calf. It's been manageable so far, so I keep going, even though the achiness is formidable, sometimes.

Athletic "Absolutes"

As mentioned throughout, my baseball career was most helpful in maintaining a work ethic beyond where others may go. Following are lessons that have helped my commitment to run and are critical messages all athletes must know.

- *It may seem overwhelming at times, but sacrifices are an avenue to improvement. When young, I could have been doing something else which required less sweat, but I chose to pass on family vacations and rise before dawn to play. Later in my career, many all-night bus rides, late-night and daybreak flights tested my resolve.* **Lesson learned — days will come when I don't want to run and prefer to join the party, but I know I can prevent self-disappointment by running.** *When the dedication to your goal is deep, sacrifice doesn't seem as severe.*

- *A key to all success is focusing on the controllable — the preparation, the concentration, and the effort. I was a consistent hard worker in my baseball career and practiced all-out searching for the elusive self-assurance.* **Lesson learned — staying focused on daily training and giving it one hundred percent is the road to confidence, or at the least, self-satisfaction.**

- *There is no way around it — the daily grind is decisive to qualify for more meaningful moments. I was fortunate to have the opportunity to play in the Los Angeles Dodgers organization. The team and front office's talent provided many chances to play postseason games. But I realized "nothing is a given," and you must earn it on the field.* **Lesson learned — missed training outings and miles will lead to the inability to finish when it counts most - the marathon.**

- *I can't say this enough, never take the games lightly and look forward to each one.* **Lesson learned — have enthusiasm for each run and treat the extended runs as a must-win playoff game.**

- *If you've played sports for any length of time, you know you are only as good as your last game. Success depends on a short memory after bad games and not becoming complacent after good ones. "Forget about it" and "Stay hungry" became my thought process.* **Lesson learned — keep the focus on incremental advancement without dwelling on the negatives or positives.** *The ten-mile mark is a confidence builder, but I know making the half marathon mark is not a given.*

- *For all athletes, misfortune and mistrust will come. I experienced many moments when demotions and a lack of advancement forced me to examine my desire. Sometimes, promotion is a matter of luck, being at the right place at the right time.* **Lesson learned — a philosophy that tomorrow will be better is the proven athlete's stance.**

Remember, the lessons never end — stay attentive!

9
The Happy Mindset

Dream Weaver

I am my younger self. After getting three hits in a row, I make an out. Devastation! And even worse, a parent (mine) keeps trying to get my attention from the stands. When I begrudgingly look over, my mom tells me to "Smile." How does one smile after it seems the world is ending?

This tale is not a dream. I learned long ago the importance of enjoying one's opportunity, to "Have fun," and realize, "It's only a game." Lesson learned, for the most part, but it's not a straightforward message to adhere to when passionate about something.

"Everything has beauty, but not everyone sees it."

Confucius

If you are not a half-full glass person, begin to think of it that way because the half-empty one runs out quicker.

121

There is little reason to work one's tail off for something you do not like. The success trail involves finding the joy in the labor, if not the love.

Stairway to success:

20. Enjoying the journey

Step Up and Enjoy the Journey

It may surprise you but my most successful season in the major leagues was one I enjoyed the least. I was happy to have the elusive productivity, but the price I had to pay did not allow me to smell the roses. It's not always easy to find pleasure when you must put a tremendous amount of energy into something.

Step twenty — finding enjoyment through inevitable frustration and disappointment. Earlier, I casually slipped in a short line, but it is nowhere near trivial. Many would say it is the central point of playing sports. The statement I glossed over, "It should be fun." That task begins with knowing one's limitations. When the athlete thinks they can do the impossible, it will be difficult to enjoy the effort.

Here's the thing; once a task becomes nothing but a struggle, and you do not look forward to the next week, you may quit. I say a week because there will be days you will not want to put in the work. **One day means little over the long haul. But if you fail to enjoy the weekly time and toil, it's time to reevaluate one's goal and perspective.** It may be necessary to take a short break, look for the "good" in the exercise, and examine your initial motives.

Find the Fun

I know a thing or two about this subject because of my thirty years of coaching. Teaching the game to youth is my intent, but helping them enjoy the practice and trials is too. Many players are hardworking and love the game, but pressures from themselves and others overwhelm them. Additionally, many are perfectionists who get down quickly to the point of losing the joy of playing.

Here are some messages I remind myself when in training and use with players to keep the playing fun. **These tips can be viewed as one of those much-needed pep talks, too.**

- Be thankful for others, skill, health, and energy. Gratitude is an overlooked source of enjoyment and motivation. Whenever my spirits were low on the ball diamond, I had to remind myself how lucky I was to be playing a kid's game as an adult. **I made sure to reflect on my past teammates, who would give everything for the opportunity I have.** I am also thankful for the understanding, patience, and assistance from many people with my pursuits. I've learned to recognize the sacrifice others made to my success and let them know their importance to my hopes. Please know that life achievements are more memorable with others. I often reflect on family, friends, teammates, and former coaches who helped and make a point to thank them.

- With that in mind, it's critical to share desires and adventures with family, friends, and co-workers, but modestly. I tried not to wear a "big league head" around when I played in the MLB. Finally, **gratitude and sharing of self and life events are in my perfect-day absolutes.**

- Take pride in the decision "to try." Someone unknown said it clearly, "The most difficult step is the first one out the door." I may not have had much confidence in my career, but I gave my all as often as possible, and I am proud of that. **Remember, regrets come from failing to act on ambitions.**

- Embrace your identity, vision, and reasons to keep at it each day with a joyful disposition. **It's comforting to see yourself in the image you want others to perceive you, and your attitude will make you a role model for others.**

- Keep expectancies reasonable. It became apparent early that becoming an All-Star was expecting too much of myself in the majors. I realized a practical outlook was doing my best each day, and **victory is the outcome of giving what you got.** If a full marathon becomes unreasonable for you, **recognize the smaller milestones. As mentioned before, a lifestyle filled with exercise makes it a worthwhile end.**

- Do not dwell on the negatives or "beat yourself up" after not getting everything you set out to do. You must be aware of what you are realistically capable of and being too harsh on yourself is the

124

quickest way to lose enjoyment. **Taking pleasure in accomplishment is necessary even when coming up short of expectations.** It's the reason players may celebrate even when down on the scoreboard.

- Frame your perception of what you do positively. If you perceive something as only sweat and pain, you are in trouble. I always tried to look at baseball practice as an opportunity and not work. I considered the effort a time of fun, independence, and exploration. **Replace a frown with a smile, and you will notice everything becomes more accessible!** I try to look at every run as a chance to shine and be free.

- Be optimistic. There is no doubt upbeat people have an advantage when striving for higher. I attribute making the big leagues to my belief in good happening to those who work and wait. When negativity arrives, pessimists often say, "What's the use," and quit. Outcomes are unpredictable, but attitude isn't. **You determine your mood, and favorable results have a better chance with a happy frame of mind.**

- Embrace the discipline a schedule demands and make self-control a habit. The baseball season and marathon training involve regularity day after day. **Having a structure to your days and weeks provides comfort and purpose many people lack.** Waking each day knowing you have something significant to do is purposeful living.

- Rejoice in every little advancement. I ask my young ballplayers to look for and enjoy skill development continually. Making the next level on the big leagues' path was always a triumph to cheer. The small wins along the way are the means to maintain enthusiasm and momentum. **I am a big believer that "a feeling of success," whether it is actual or not, is necessary for desire, so make a toast to you as you gain miles.**

Create Your Beauty

Another critical ingredient for fun is noticing the beauty in one's surroundings as pleasure comes through the eyes. Professional baseball took me to neat places, but at times, I had to remind myself to be aware of the cities' sights and sounds. Sometimes I catch myself staring at the ground right in front of me when jogging, but I know better. Setting eyes on the worms and earth makes the run less enjoyable. When the eyes look up, beauty surrounds me. I know that makes sense because life and running are delightful when we look ahead and take in the world around us. Extraordinary views help to provide distractions for the mind to wander and wonder. **As you appreciate the magnificence around you, life's paths are more enjoyable.**

Of all the things I enjoy about running, the contentment that arrives from being creative is the most satisfying. Enjoyment comes from letting one's mind run free, and **running provides the perfect opportunity to think and create.** A quote from *Born to Run* says, *"If you don't have answers to your problems after a four-hour run, you ain't getting them."* I agree because I haven't figured out any yet. Until I do, I will keep moving, searching for, and building the world I want.

Here are some examples of the mind's creativity from eye-catching surroundings:

· I come around a bend on one of my regular trails, and the **Chicago skyline appears**. It's inspiring moments like this, like finding a new world, that is priceless. I imagine big things ahead for me, the country, and the world.

· I come upon a **lighthouse**. The sight provides hope all is not lost, and I then know I can finish the run. I long for the light to shine through our prejudices and put an end to our tunnels of hatred.

· I pass **a pond** and feel a serenity of doing things I love, like running. I believe I see the reflection of God's presence in my being and the world. I pray for pure hearts and peace on earth!

· The power of **Lake Michigan's waves** reminds me of the relentless pursuit of the finish line. I see the waves of liberty and prosperity coming, only to recede again and again. I vow to speak for freedom!

· **Airplanes** remind me to keep my head high through the tough stretches. They remind me to look beyond oneself to the heavens and to keep believing in God, humankind, and goodness!

· In uninspiring areas, I imagine dashing on some remote canyons, hills, and valleys. I appear light of foot, head held high with worldly troubles far away. Also, I picture myself on the course of a marathon I want to run but may never.

And on and on, the mind goes. **Joy comes from the imagination, inspired by a vision to create a beautiful existence. It is blissful when the endorphins brought on by exercise produce the spectacular.**

A Marathon Legend Capsule

Just Do It

This athlete loved competing so much, and he never let anything stop him from it.

I've written about the necessity of reading about inspirational people before heading out for an extended run. Stories help with that extra something to occupy the mind and a push when most needed. The following story is a great example.

The year was 1960, and I remember October 13th of that year as if it were yesterday. At my cousin's house watching the 7th game of the World Series, I see Bill Mazeroski's championship homerun. I'm sure the viewing played a role in my dream of becoming a major league player. A little over a month before that day, the 1960 Rome Olympic games occurred, the one in which Muhamad Ali, then Cassius Clay, won a boxing gold medal.

In those Games, another remarkable athlete won the Marathon, Abebe Bikila. How awesome was he, you might ask? Well, as if winning a gold medal is not notable enough, two months before the Olympic games, Bikila ran his first Marathon. He won and followed that with another marathon the next month in a world record time. For his third Marathon in three months, he set another world record in the Olympic Games and did it barefoot. After wearing some ill-fitted shoes before the Marathon, the ensuing blisters forced him to run without them. After the race, he began touching his toes and running in place

129

and said he could have run another six to nine miles. What? That is not human. Four years later, he became the first runner to repeat as marathon winner in the Olympics in the 1964 Tokyo Olympics.

The rest of Bikila's story is a little sad and yet just as incredible. After becoming paralyzed from a car accident, he never walked again. As implied, that is not the end of the story. A year after the accident, in 1970, Bikila participated in wheelchair games in archery, table tennis, and cross-country sled dog racing.

His exemplary life inspires many lessons for all. The main one is what makes one an athlete – the ability to adjust to what sports and life throw at you. Blisters, no problem — run barefoot. Paralyzed, no big deal — find another sport. The competitor finds a way! Unfortunately, the story ended way too early as Bikila died in 1973 at age 41 from a cerebral hemorrhage. Gone, but not forgotten, another sign of greatness.

My Story: High and Not so High

There are places I'll remember

All my life though, some have changed

Some forever, not for better

Some have gone, and some remain

Beatles *"In My Life"*

Searching

Finding the "Baseball High" was easy. The lofty feeling came with merely imagining the start of Spring Training, a new season, and each game. The joy of playing and competing created a unique sensation. Equally, playing along and against some all-time greats in baseball history was a dream that never got old. The bat's sound, the fans, and stealing a base also contributed to an elevated consciousness. Added to all that, the relationships, daily work ethic, personal achievement, and winning brought enjoyment. I must admit I miss those things to this day.

Unlike my baseball bliss, I must keep searching for that state of exhilaration on the longer-running treks. Don't get me wrong, I love to run, but I want the state of mind known as the "Runner's High." One definition says it's "a feeling of euphoria with less anxiety and diminished pain." It is supposed to show after many exercise miles and sounds fabulous.

Euphoria, no anxiety or pain — now we're talking. Who wouldn't want to find that drug out on the course? To have feel-good chemicals circulating and ready to party would be desirable any time after mile 15. I usually have happiness early in the long run. But, to say I've ever had each ingredient after several miles would not be accurate. Unless I wasn't paying attention, the sense of ecstasy has only been a dream unfulfilled. I have had two-thirds of the high, but one of the three has always been absent. Maybe it's my age?

Some say the runner's high comes after the long run. If a cheeseburger and a beer fit the bill, then, on second thought, I have had the high. And, although it may not be the rapture, a comfortable result, that of a state of uncommon relaxation lives after a long hike. It's an extreme state of leisure, where no amount of coaxing by a family member can get me to move. I hope you experience this peaceful state as I have because it's a world of your own.

Deserving

Here is the point. Whenever I consider my enormous number of running hours, it's not too much to ask for that elevated rush. I have paid my dues, I believe. What's a guy to do to have the Runners High? So be it. Just knowing it's out there somewhere makes it worth the effort to keep going far. I must keep searching for the high, especially with the unlikely return of an MLB career.

Now, what I have had is "The Runner's Low" — the situation of painful brainwaves, inquiries of this ever

ending, and why am I doing this? Additionally, back, leg, neck aches, blisters, and boredom live on, all things that lower one's drive.

As you might recognize, long-distance running mimics life in that way. Even though many good times exist, the struggles require ninety percent of our thoughts and energy. Oh well.

10

The Winner's Mindset

A Dream Come True

This game has been going on forever. A regular game is nine innings, but this one is in the seventeenth. Almost two games, and neither team can score. I get a chance, and I come through by knocking in the go-ahead run. Memorable, yes, but even more so because it occurred in the "House that Ruth Built," Yankee Stadium. Dreams do not get much better than that for a ballplayer. Please, do not let me wake!

Occasionally, things go according to plan.

"It's at the borders of pain and suffering that the men are separated from the boys." **Emil Zatopek**

By mile 14, those borders close in on you. I'm sure Emil Zatopek, a respectful man, would have included, "Women are separated from the girls" in today's times.

The success trail gets exciting with the end in sight, but only those, who know how to turn it on, get the satisfaction they want.

Stairway to success:

21. Adaptation

22. Closing

3rd Month Training Steps — Miles 13 – 17

Turn the Corner

Making the half marathon distance was like playing sports at the college level. Hard work and sacrifice went into the voyage, but nothing compared to what was to follow. At the professional level, baseball became a full-time, 365 day a year job, and advancing in the minor league chain was an enormous test. Passing miles after thirteen is, too. Moving beyond 13.1 miles means the final exam is getting close, but so much more study is necessary.

Life and sports are not all about winning, even though it may be that way for some. **A higher purpose exists or should, and each person must decide their aim.** Yet, if one gets the choice of being a winner or not, one hundred out of a hundred athletes would choose to win. Why is that? Winners hold their heads a little higher, and success enhances life's purpose. Many things contribute to winning, not the least of those being talent. A plan, work ethic, dedication, perseverance, and even luck, play a role. **A recipe for defeat is believing you know it all and being unwilling to change.**

Step twenty-one - the willingness and ability to adapt. For the athlete, the alterations involve the ever-changing body and mind. Winning takes a constant and honest evaluation, and using one's past to figure out the required adaptations is the start. Even after training for many marathons, an analysis must occur because the challenge to remain healthy and be more efficient is ever-present.

Review the Way

Successful people review their preparation and practice procedures by:

- Attending to the minutest details

- Using experience and instincts to revise their actions and intellect

- Changing the process when necessary to get where they need to be

You will find marathon training is a constant battle of adjusting to the roller coaster of emotions and effort. As mentioned before, no rhyme or reason is apparent in sports. You will need continual adjustments because one week of runs go smoothly, and the following week not so much. Some runs during the week are like a cool breeze, and the next seems the year's first run. Often, tremendous energy and optimism occur initially but then disappear around the corner. The emotional turbulence continues with dreading today's run, and it turns into a lovely cruise. One must make many trips to the drawing board to review performance and training habits.

Here is the necessary self-interrogation to discover when change is needed:

✓ Am I staying with the weekly schedule? **Remember, shortcuts are for losers. If you scrimp, it will bite you later.**

✓ Am I doing the little things to win the day's activity? Eating and hydrating the days and hours before hitting the trail is an ongoing mission. If you fail to do either before any sizable run, it will lead to excessive labor. **Most importantly, a healthy, everyday lifestyle makes running and recovery better.**

✓ Is my pre-run attitude helping or hurting my chances? **It's vital to psyche up and play every game as if it were the last one.**

✓ Am I drinking and snacking enough on the course? **Too little intake in action can be a run-stopper, also.** Whenever I have consumed less with the intent of avoiding restroom stops, it proved an amateur mistake.

✓ Is my pace too fast in the beginning? **Early speed can do a lot of harm later, so keep an eye on your watch, as it is easy to overdo the initial stretch.**

✓ Have I prepared some mind-diversions for the dreary miles? **Because of the "craziness" of sports performance, be aware the most demanding phase can show up early, middle, or late in the run.**

✓ Am I religious about cross-training to build back the muscle strength? Running alone is not enough to keep one steady and ready for the long runs. Strengthening the areas around one's core, hips, and shins is invaluable. **The exciting news is cross-training also creates valued self-discipline and confidence.**

✓ Why did I struggle this time? The answer to this never-ending predicament comes from a **review of the slightest details.**

Unfortunately, sometimes there are no answers for why one succeeds or fails from one day to the next. But the effort to find out should never stop because one never knows when clues will show. **No matter how minor, finding any change offers hope and determination.**

Adjust or Go Home

After figuring out what needs to happen for improvement, one must do it. After the half marathon distance, thoughts about the pain and miles make the time seem eternal. The athlete knows they must make the change happen because no one can do it for them.

Former World Champion boxer, Mike Tyson, said, "Everyone has a plan until they get punched in the mouth." The same applies in a marathon, although it's not a literal punch. It may seem like one, and how you react after the blow leads to becoming a winner. **The winning mindset begins with shaping one's demeanor in the heat of the moment.** It's not always an easy thing to do when one's spirit is low, and why winning is hard to do. But the belief in the mind's power to make things happen makes it possible.

138

The mind's framing begins with more positive self-talk. The following are some motivational statements I use. It helps to say them out loud and repeat them during the run when every ounce of you wants to stop.

When an edge is needed, repeat these:

- "I work when others don't."

- "I love a challenge."

- "I may get tired, but I don't get beat."

- "I got this,"

- "I will own this mile."

- "I believe in me."

- "I won't stop until I'm proud."

Close It Out

When things get dire on the sport's field, some players shy away from the moment and others "want it." Another key to winning is playing with no fear of failure and desiring the ball and action at the game's end. If you are of the first sort, you must begin the process of converting to the second group — one who wants the game-winning shot or to be up to the plate with the game on the line. It's critical to know playing with nerves is good, but playing with fear is not.

Step twenty-two — knowing when and how to turn it on and close things out. Many people slack off or do not know how to finish, and they do not achieve what they set out to do. But the victorious can taste the finish line and apply themselves like there is no tomorrow near the end. The ability to add focus once the destination is in sight is a sure sign of the winner. Those who do not win have a first, second, and third gear, but the champ can turn to a 4th. **Once putting forth more comes without forcing it, and you know it is what you "must do," you have what it takes.**

Takeaways from Month Three

1. The mental and physical battle begins in full rage around mile 14; it's how you adapt to it that makes or breaks the event.

2. The winner studies and applies their experience. There are always new conditions to figure out, and failing to learn from the past opens the door for repeated mistakes, which is a sure path to losing.

3. Ongoing reviews find the little details that lead to adaptation.

4. The mind is an unbelievably powerful mechanism, and it can "will" one to finish.

5. Finding a way to close it out is the difference between getting there and "almost."

6. Positive self-talk is urgent as the going gets tough.

In the end, how do you know you are a winner? You use the struggle to make you better the next time.

A Marathon Legend Capsule

To Die For

This athlete knew what it meant to "come to play," whether he knew how great a runner he was or not. He was a winner of the first marathon and a hero, too.

One must be "Bigtime" when remembered over two thousand years later, and I am not talking about someone most of us know, who I pray to, often. That is a story for another book. But a man born in 530 BC would be proud to know he became a legend. Unfortunately, I suppose, neither man had the chance to see their one-day, universal fame.

Hold on to your seats; there was a time when there was no phone communication of any sort. News traveled by word of mouth, period. Legend has it that an Athenian named Pheidippides had the task of informing his countrymen of a war victory in Marathon. His travel means were not a plane, train, or auto, but stepping it out quickly. The distance was around twenty-five miles, and the area of Marathon became synonymous with running a far-way on foot.

The marathon name seems fitting, with the other possibilities being his name, Pheidippides, and imagine saying that. Other options were Running a Persian or an Acropolis, so we are fortunate, I suppose. For the rest of the story, the young herald died upon reaching the destination. I would never make light of death, especially when thinking about the first marathon winner, but I am not surprised by his outcome. Even with months of training, the distance is daunting, as written many times here, so hats off to Pheidippides, a Hero, no doubt, for delivering the welcome news. Supposedly, his last words were, "Joy, we win." I know the feeling when finishing a marathon, and my words are, "Thank God, that is over, and I'm alive." Sorry Pheidippides, just kidding.

I've also written of the difficulty of being the first to do something, and he exemplified that well. A couple of thousand years later, his feat became forever immortalized with the running of marathons worldwide and the first Olympic one in 1896.

My Story: Pep Talk

"Well you better start swimming or sink like a stone

For the times they are a-changin ...

For the loser now

Will be later to win

For the times they are a-changin'

Bob Dylan *"The Times they are A Changin"*

Adaptation

Performing to standards at the professional level was a constant battle. There was always someone just as talented or more ready to take my spot. The ever-present worry of release or demotion never allowed much relaxation. I knew the career could end at any time and feared getting stuck at the same level, a telling sign of the end. What was the solution to not getting stuck? Adaptability. And it had to continue after making it to the top, or failure loomed. The players who stay in the major leagues for more than a "cup of coffee" adjust, while the resistors may only get one taste. Many athletes struggle because they repeat mistakes, either out of obstinance or ignorance.

Every off-season, I analyzed and put extra work on my weaknesses from the season. Some years it was on the offensive side and others on the defensive. In season, continual daily assessment and development were central to success. Few areas of sports require adjusting as hitting a baseball does. It's a cat and mouse game where the batter must try to figure out how the pitcher is attempting to get them out pitch after pitch. My first go-around in the big leagues forced a needed adjustment after discovering I could not consistently get the bat's sweet spot on the ball. I had to find a new approach if I was going to have a chance of getting back to that level and stick around. I decided to choke up on the bat. This adjustment worked, and it led to consistent, solid contact. The lesson is why, as a coach, I try to convince players of the necessity of being willing to try new things.

The teams, coaches, and players I had the fortune to be with taught me about winning. Two critical aspects of coming out on top were increased focus and positive visualization at the end of games. All distractions took a back seat, especially late in games, and my mind would be in the moment, all the while picturing being the hero at the game's end. I also figured out how to prepare with concentrated practice and higher motivation the days before playoff games. It's essential to know a successful closing is within you.

Closing the Race

In training, I continually examine the process, get "fired up" to run, adapt on the fly, and close it out once I smell the finish line. Even though I often find myself saying, "No "effin" way I have twenty-six miles in me," I know there is a way. And when the answers seem elusive, I go back to the drawing board and examine all aspects for improvement. I also apply things learned in baseball, which taught me the mind's remarkable ability to adapt.

For example, although I played with little confidence in my career, in high-pressure game moments, I felt comfortable.

There is little doubt the mental game is the determining factor for going beyond what one thinks they can. Near the end of long runs, I fight to get to the end, despite how I may feel. Winners close it out, and that is what I want to be. As proof of the mind's ability, on the day the schedule calls for 12 miles, I seem to have that amount of energy. If it's 15, I have enough to complete it even though finishing half that amount the time before was brutal. It's incredible how the mind rises, and it is what being an athlete is.

Another helpful thing is the mantras I have developed for the arduous runs. One mantra I use is the same one I give my hitting students to help relax them and put them in the moment. RBI, a baseball term for runs batted in, is easy to recall. With running, it stands for Relax, Breathe, Improve, instead. Another of my favorites, Pace, Focus, Confidence. I have many more, and it's fun to create catchy sayings when out running with the number of possibilities endless.

11
The Acclimating Mindset

Not A Dream

My family is afraid. They can't reach me and set out in cars to find me. Why? An unexpected thunderstorm hit, and I am out running in it.

If you haven't had the above happen to you, wait. I've had my game plan fall apart because of Mother Nature and my decision-making on many occasions. The lesson is obvious – do not put all your trust in the weather or the weather prognosticator. Also, it is worth it to alter your schedule to confirm safety and avoid annoying family members.

"Rain hangs about the place, like a friendly ghost. if it's not coming down in delicate droplets, then it's in buckets; and if neither, it tends to lurk suspiciously in the atmosphere."

Barbara Acton-Bond

It pays to be aware of any suspicious lurking.

The success trail is about taking advantage of the situations that present themselves while knowing one false move can be detrimental.

Stairway to success:

23. Acclimation

"Weathering" through the Playing Conditions

Step twenty-three — using the playing conditions to one's advantage. Athletes must prepare so the "unexpected" doesn't beat them to the point of no return. A good start is to read about the marathon you signed up for, so you are not surprised by any circumstances. I have a friend whose first marathon was the Big Sur marathon, which he entered for the beauty it possesses. What he forgot to consider was the constant up and downhill climbs. It was a hearty exam, and it deterred him from wanting to run another after it. Another detail to consider is the weather. You cannot start this plea too early - pray for clear and sixty degrees on marathon day. And, along with the appeal, you may as well ask for light or no wind.

So, I have done some research! One source calculates the ideal long-distance temperature is between 44 and 59 degrees. I would lean towards the second of those temps, but anything in that range is a plus. Studies say the amount of oxygen used in warm weather is much more considerable than in the cold. Without going into the exact scientific data, heat sucks the energy out of you. When you add in high humidity to heat, it's double the trouble. Extreme cold is another instance not to mess with, and ice and snow conditions are a no-go.

Good Decision Tips

The trouble with many parts of the country is the lack of five months of fine training weather, so most runners must prepare for uncomfortable conditions. You may have other guidelines based on your area and the time of year. Each person's body acclimates to hot and cold weather differently, so find what works for you. It pays to be wise when dealing with the weather because one wrong decision can lead to an unhealthy conclusion. Dressing in layers is a good plan, so you can add and subtract clothing as needed. Instead of risking your health and not working out, a treadmill or indoor track is a solution. Below are some weather tips to be aware of:

- Check the seven-day forecast. Although not always reliable, it will help avoid missed runs. The weather outlook mainly aids in scheduling your long run day, with the **warning it is hard to get psyched for an alternate day at the last minute, so an educated plan is essential.**

- Do not put complete trust in a forecast, even one from the night before. Experience informs me it's worth checking a weather application before leaving the house for the hourly forecast and becoming adept at analyzing the radar. As implied, a lot can change in a short period, so assume nothing.

- Never mess with thunder and lightning. **There may be no safe place if a storm busts out, so it pays to play it safe when one is possible.**

- Rain is a problem of varying degrees. I would advise you not to head far from home if it is imminent unless it is the light variety. Once your clothes and shoes get drenched, no fun ensues. Appropriate apparel — a brimmed hat, a rain jacket, and cell phone protection — should be part of your wardrobe and can save you from an early shower.

- Avoid high heat and humidity for extended runs. **As mentioned, temperatures and humidity levels above 75 make things dangerous.** Just one of those zaps your energy enough, and together they are total burnouts. On the first sign of overheating, stop or stroll until feeling better. When I head out on torrid days, I will alternate walking and running each block. According to my assessment, the one saving grace is finishing in extreme weather equals double the mileage in average temperatures.

- It is worth noting it's often heat-related whenever a death occurs in a marathon. Investing in cooling towels for your neck may help, and psychologically, too. Hydrate even more than usual, even if it means circling back to the house every few miles to get liquids. It helps to drink extra before and after the run, too, as it is hard to overdo the hydration. But be sure to factor in more restroom stops from drinking more.

- Cold is rarely a run negator if you dress right, but that is not always easy. Keep in mind the body will warm a few miles into your run, and you may want to shed clothing. Yet, after a while, your body temperature can dip, and sweat can make you cold, which may lead to shivering and danger. The lower body temperatures are the reason some marathons give out warming HeetSheets at the end. If any skepticism about needing them, gloves and headbands are easy to transport, so take them.

- Snow and ice are conditions not to mess with, ever. Be aware the latter of those can be unseen until it's too late. As always, if there is any doubt of safety, take the cautionary route and exercise indoors.

- Use sunscreen even in colder and slightly cloudy weather. I'm always amazed at the toll the sun can have when it's least expected. A sun-shielding hat is a good weapon.

- Calculate the high wind direction. My advice in higher winds, obvious I know, is to take a route where it's at your back when finishing. But on warm days with medium wind, having it in the face can be soothing for the finishing miles. Your choice. The surprising thing is that above-average winds are not necessarily a deterrent because it works both ways. The less energy expended while it's at your back balances the opposite. **Of course, stopped-in-your tracks wind is a day to run indoors.**

As a final reminder, non-stop days of rain, ice, or high heat can disrupt training, so an indoor alternative is necessary.

A Marathon Legend Capsule

The Best

To be in the conversation of the best-ever is fantastic itself.

As with most activities, naming someone "the best-ever" is subjective. It isn't easy to compare different generations, especially when training methods, equipment, and playing conditions improve with time. I am of the disposition the "greats" would be in any era, as they would find a way to meet the times' criteria. The same subjectiveness applies to runners. For example, one source lists one athlete as the greatest, and another says someone different. With that in mind, the following are two of the most productive runners, knowing they happen to be the ones that caught my eye, and I am leaving many others out.

A Simple Woman

We all know athletes are big, solid, and muscular behemoths easily discernable. They intimidate people with their power. Then, there is one of the greatest athletes ever, all five-foot-two-inch, 99-pound Rosa Mota. Rosa shows athletes come in all shapes and sizes and dominate not with their size but with their guts.

Despite having asthma as a child and later sciatica, Rosa rose to become one of the elite female marathon runners. Over twelve years, she ran 21 marathons and won 14 of them. Mota was intimidating, after all. After finishing second in the 1984 Olympic Games, she won the 1988

151

ones, the first Portuguese athlete to win a gold medal. Rosa won the Chicago marathon twice, but ironically her personal best time of 2:23.49 was only good for third place. The math says her time comes out to a 5 minute, 47-second pace per mile for 26.2 miles – incredible.

Two other things struck me when reading about Rosa. The day after finishing second in the 1984 Olympics, she began working for the next Olympics. Are you kidding me? Most runners can't move the next day and despise the thought of getting out there again that soon. It's what makes one a champion, I suppose. Secondly, Rosa said this when describing herself years later, "I'm a simple woman who worked hard." It's hard not to like someone so good when they are so humble and genuine.

All Haile

Like others I've written, it's always unique to hear how some people become world-famous after such modest, if not horrible, beginnings. Haile Gebrselassie was another example, as he was one of ten kids born in **Asella**, Ethiopia. Haile ran six miles to school each day and the same back. Having to transport books on the journey, he developed a running style where his left arm crooked as if holding books.

The thing that stands out most when reading of him was his versatility. Haile broke world records, an astonishing 27 in all, and won gold medals at various distances ranging from 5000 meters to the Marathon. His tremendous speed at shorter distances paid off when he eventually moved into running the 26.2-mile races. At the age of 35, he set one of those world records in the Berlin

Marathon. Not only was it the world record at the time, but his world record stood for many years longer for the Master's age group.

The most important lesson I take away from reading about Haile is, "When you can, you owe it to yourself to do."

My Story: History Repeats

"I run and run as the rains come,

And I look up, I look up,

On my knees and out of luck, I look...

But I won't rot, I won't rot,

Not his mind and not this heart, I won't rot."

Mumford and Sons *"After the Storm"*

Mother Nature

History is a confusing thing, but it's critical we pay attention and learn from it. This story is how it happened many years ago, and one that circles back to me many years later.

I was on the mighty Albuquerque Dukes, the Los Angeles Dodgers Triple-A team from 1979 - 1981. Please take my word for it; using the term mighty is not an exaggeration. Our 1981 squad was among the best minor league teams ever. And, our 1979 and 1980 teams may have been even better, but the MLB strike year of 1981 prevented call-ups, so the players stayed put.

In the game I write of, we were doing what Dukes do – rule. After three and a half innings, we were winning by a considerable margin. Even though an afternoon game, one would not know it because of the imminent storm and the bright stadium lights. It's worth knowing with the desert ground so hard, any downpour created huge puddles. Even with a tarp, the field often became unplayable after a quick soaking.

It looked dark for our opponent and the skies as they turned black. However, in baseball, a game is not official until the visiting team gets up to bat for five innings. We needed to get through our half inning and retire their side in the fifth. So, to be sure our lead and efforts would not go to waste, we devised a plan to move it along. Of course, the opposing team's manager knows the situation, so he countered.

With the time precious, our manager had players strike out on purpose. This plan being apparent, the opposing coach strolled out to the mound and changed pitchers. Our next batter followed orders, striking out by not swinging the bat to get to two outs. Their manager returned to the mound for further delay and instructed their catcher to let the third strike go past from now on, so the runner would go to first safely. Yes, this set up a no-win situation for either side.

Looking back, it was a hilarious scene, as evidenced by the fans, and even many players, roaring with laughter. Striking out on purpose and a catcher refusing to catch were bizarre sights. After this farce of a professional game, the umpire had enough. He met with the managers to bring order to the situation, thank God. I'm sure you know where this is going. Despite the sky's ominous nature, not a drop of rain came. To our dismay, our opponent came charging back, and we lost the game. This crazy outcome emphasizes points made earlier – sports are unpredictable, it's never over until it's official, and do not trust mother nature.

The Rest of His-Story

That fun memory was the first thing I thought of as my running day unfolded. The night before a run of 13 miles, I see the weather forecast of temperatures in the afternoon of high 80's and humidity. That outlook necessitates my getting up early to beat some of the heat. Early morning temperatures were to be in the low 70's, which would make the run more doable. I planned to be out the door by 6:30 and home by 9 to get to church.

The best-laid plans disappeared upon waking; it was much darker outside than expected. Uh-oh! I checked the weather app, and wouldn't you know it, a storm beginning in seven minutes and staying for a while. Radar showed all yellow and green colors. The message was clear — go back to bed. Light rain would not deter a run, but the heavy stuff and storms are never worth testing.

With things out of my control, it's back to sleep. Of course, you know the rest of the story again — no precipitation all morning. "How does that happen?" I wonder. Being a runner, competitor, and occasionally stupid, I felt there was no choice but to take off in the afternoon heat. Here's the thing; the thirteen-mile run was as harsh as any marathon I have run. Semi-delirious near the end, it took all my willpower to finish. The funny thing was I ended up praying twice as much as in the morning church service. As often happens with distance running, this question comes, how does a lesser amount -

13 miles, in this case, seem like 30. The answer, in this case, is simple — heat can be a killer.

Suffice it to say, the mentality of going for it, no matter the circumstances, is the athlete's curse. We feel we can overcome anything, and the show must go on. In this instance, I paid for the usually-advantageous athletic character trait of tenacity. It was another reminder that Mother Nature is unpredictable and rules like the Dukes. Add it to the learned lesson department — sound decisions backfire occasionally, and that's the way it goes. It's time to move on a little wiser.

12
The "In the Zone" Mindset

Day Dreaming

I'm passing by with my cape on with a massive S on the front of my shirt. I am not faster than a speeding bullet or unable to leap tall buildings, but? At a busy, four-way intersection, an older man falls mid-crossing and cannot get up. Many people gasp as I, but I spring to action and help him out of harm's way. On another run, I pass a family with young kids. Their daughter accidentally drops her soccer ball, and it moves towards a bustling street. As God would have it, I scoop the ball in stride as she began to dart after it. Her parents were grateful, as was I, for being in the right place at the right time.

These events happened. Sometimes one is in the zone, reacts instinctively, and everything clicks precisely right. When you must be more than your athletic prowess, take on a superhero role! It's admirable to look out for your neighbor. With that in mind, a friendly gesture is to check on hurting runners and provide a little emotional support. It's something I appreciate when I am struggling. Best of all, when you help another, it often comes back to you when most needed.

"Never let the body tell the mind what to do. The body will always give up ... But the body is never tired if the mind is not tired."

General George Patton

When a general speaks, one must listen.

Ultimately, the success trail's determining factor comes down to getting the mind to a mental state where nothing can deter it from the necessary focus. It's not an easy thing, but it's a game-changing moment.

Stairway to success:

24. The Zone

4th Month Training Steps — Miles 18 -22

Find your Groove in the Dog Days

I intend no disrespect here; dogs are my favorite animal, and I didn't invent the Dog Days phrase. But for those who have a dog, you understand. You're walking your dog on a hot day, and she decides she's had enough. Yep, she sits, and all the coaxing in the world will not change her mind to move until she is good and ready.

Why am I talking about dog walking? A terrific chance exists that you will feel like your "Man's Best Friend" at this point in training. You and your dog are "one" in demeanor because you will want to sit a lot, and any inclination to move will have little chance. In the fourth month, the high number of miles put you into the "weary hound" training period.

For non-dog people, it's this. You have been toiling along for what feels forever, with no end in sight, and the mind and body drain is severe. There will be times you want to lay on the couch for hours, and every action takes longer to start and finish. Instead of taking a five-minute shower, it turns into a fifteen-minute one. Instead of mowing the grass today, you justify putting it off until tomorrow.

Fight through the Make-or-Break Time

The last month of training requires a resolve you will question even more than before. You will be putting in at least 40 miles per week at this training juncture. It's the final training trial to see if you have what it takes to run a marathon. The good news is if you can hang in there a few more weeks, a light at the tunnel's end awaits. **The other good news is you will be only a marathon finish away from becoming a hero.**

An excellent start to getting through is to believe that you are an athletic Superstar. For proof this time, ask a professional athlete if they want to accompany you on a twenty-mile trek. Their response will probably be priceless. With no uncertainty, upon finishing 20 miles, you are a superstar. You should not count on having the energy to celebrate that status, though.

By mile 18, the zapped energy levels affect the body and mind. A big problem is a pointed menace appears now, if not before this. I purposely did not mention this in the section on-road dangers, but it is **a severe hazard —**

boredom. Once it arrives, the miles and minutes can seem forever and cause you to stop. Even minor body pain can be better than boredom because your mind has the ache to dwell on. The two together take every bit of tenacity to keep going.

Step twenty-four — finding the zone, a carefree state of mind that leads to ultimate focus. There is no getting around the weariness dragging on you now, so you must find a way to eliminate the monotony and pain. The phrase "getting in the zone" is playing without focusing on process, expectations, or outcome. The athlete operates freely and gains a concentration beyond the average player. **Getting in the zone is a level reserved for only a select few, and you must believe you are one of the chosen ones.**

Manufacture the Zone

If nothing else, know that your ability to focus on anything but the pain, doubt, and boredom will be the determining factor to finish. Some days finding the zone comes without coaxing; other times, it takes effort, and it may never arrive. The latter of those is the most defiant outings and the runs that tax you into wanting to walk or stop. When the zone may come is another of the sports-playing mysteries. I can tell you that finding the place where time and effort do not exist can improve with practice.

It's worth noting some runners do not need outside stimuli because they focus on their movements and each step. More power to them, but I cannot do that, at least for long. Others focus on an object in the distance to put their mind on something besides the work. Once again, it is not something I can do for long. I do the opposite **and get my mind a million miles away from each step.** It helps to have a prominent issue or two going on in your life to help fritter away the time, and who doesn't. But spending your time figuring out even the gravest problems will not fill all the minutes.

Here are some **zone-making tips to** put the mind in a relaxed, focused state.

* Find inspiration before the long jogs by reading about genius people or finding fascinating podcasts. A little preparation goes a long way.

* Remind yourself how much you love to run and that you would not trade it for anything. Once again, framing the mind with optimism is a difference-maker.

* Use visualization skills. Visualization could easily have been a step itself, but I've included it under the zone section because it's putting the mind in a different place. High-end athletes use it all the time to see themselves performing, and it is a prerequisite for high performance. **In a marathon, it's all about the image of being on the course and closing it out.**

* Show confidence whether you feel it or not. Self-assurance can be elusive, but having the look of control can make it so. The thing to know is that **feeling ready aids relaxation, which is a critical factor in making the zone possible.**

* Let the mind wander. Two, three, and even four hours to fill the mind can be a massive task. Another of the

roads to the zone is daydreaming. Daydreaming facilitates the miles to pass with fewer thoughts of the miles to go, which is the goal, of course. For more of the relaxed state, I see myself sunning on a beach, hitting a hole in one, and helping others. **A mental picture of things one loves can get the mind far from what they are doing.** Sometimes, I picture myself loping alongside some historic marathon runners, like Eliud Kipchoge and Haile Gebrselassie. Just trying to spell and pronounce their names can get you through a few miles, I joke. I also think of good days, family members, special friends, and memorable sporting events.

Once again, having as many things as possible to contemplate before heading out should be part of your plan. **And a state of mindlessness — when the mind is free of worry, results, pain, and negative brainwaves, is the place you want to be**.

Share Your Time

Another helpful course of action is a running buddy or group. Traveling with others enables discussion, which assists in passing the time. **Partners can push each other when it's most imperative, too.** In my Hawaii marathon, I was fortunate to have my son alongside to commiserate and keep me going. He could have gone ahead but chose to hang with me because he realized I wasn't having the best of it.

Dance to the Music

Listening to exciting stuff on headphones can be a zone-finding difference-maker, too. I recommend wireless to avoid the hassle of wires, but the wire ones suffice. Listening possibilities include podcasts, live or recorded radio shows, audible books, and music. Many genres exist with them, and you can mix the options. Any interesting material can occupy the mind for long stretches. You can also talk to friends and family by phone if desired. **And a tip from earlier, save the most magnetic material for the miles when monotony is most prominent.**

You could not have missed the many musical references here to indicate how vital music is to me. I believe music is another of my absolutes for a perfect day. Soulful lyrics bring me to reflect on life's past, present, and future. **Great songwriters say things in ways that clarify existence and mood.** It is advantageous to layout a playlist before starting because it can be frustrating to find tunes that captivate you when not wanting to pause.

Another ingredient for a perfect day and a diversionary tactic I use is prayer. **Summoning a higher being refreshes me, and the miles to finish go by with less consternation.** I'm always astonished by how my being relaxes and the steps seem lighter after prayer. Just me, I suppose, but worth a try for everyone. Although the urge is to pray for finishing the run, I pray for friends, family, and world betterment. OK, I admit maybe a little bit of prayer time is for the perseverance to keep moving, too.

Some runners want to get away from technology, which is understandable. If that is the case, word games, singing, work preparation, and speeches, among other things, can captivate the time. Once again, go with what works for you, but plan because boredom is a threat to keep going.

Develop a Change-Up

In my experience, another way to beat boredom is to change the program.

Here are some of my change-up strategies:

- Road trip. If you do not have any travel intentions, find well-known, new running paths a short driving distance away. Beauty is everywhere, and it can energize you to have different surroundings.

- Vary the route by going the opposite way of ordinary. Instead of going south to the Shedd Aquarium and the impressive city skyline, I go north on Lake Shore Drive. I run past Loyola and Northwestern Universities for an intelligent change if you catch my meaning.

- Change the time of day from normal. Even though my preference is late afternoon jogs, occasionally, I leave before sunset and have the world to myself. **Moving from darkness to daylight seems to shorten the longer runs, and the sunrises can be sweet.**

- Take along different energy drinks and snacks from ordinary. It's worth knowing that a minor change can be enough to add enthusiasm.

- A treadmill workout is a distinct change and gives a higher appreciation for outdoor treks. You will find that increased speed and incline work are easy adjustments on machines, too, and are the only reason I like treadmill workouts.

- If a solo runner, find someone to go with, and if a pack person, go it alone. Positives and negatives exist for jogging with others. The plus side includes companionship, discussion, motivation, and accountability. The downside is finding others who run your pace, no alone time, and annoying cohorts. A few years, I did some of my training with others, and I enjoyed it. But mostly, the solitude of traveling alone and the chance to get away from the world fits me. **Also, I consider writing my companion, medicine you may want to consider.** Pondering entries for a diary, blog, or book stimulates, distracts, and energizes.

- Instead of a usual steady-paced run, for a drastic change, have a day of sprints or uphill runs for a literal steep test. Still, other outings combine both of those for a very dynamic exercise day. The fast and upward movements build strength and stamina, along with an uplifting and powerful spirit. **Going fast is exhilarating and going higher gives one a sense of attaining something worthwhile.** Another benefit of those is your regular speed will seem to be much less work the next run.

I consider the sprints and uphill treks a graphic of the marathon itself. The first few intervals clear the mind and stretch the muscles like the early marathon miles. The following few excursions bring soreness, but the mind and body still feel confident. The last sprints and climbs push the limits. They are like the marathon end — bent over, gasping for breath, and asking, "Why am I doing this?"

166

A necessary word of caution, though. Be careful of overdoing speed and incline workouts. A higher chance of injury exists, not something you can afford. Although my sprint speed is nowhere near when I stole bases, it has led to muscle pulls and fatigue.

Takeaways from Month Four

- This segment of training tests you to the core of your commitment. It takes a herculean effort to run upwards of 40 miles for four straight weeks. The key now is stressing you didn't come this far to turn back.

- The dog days of training are finite, so take comfort in knowing a "breather" is around the corner.

- Finding methods to put your mind "in the zone" will mean continuing or quitting.

- Going fast and up can break the training monotony and have the benefit of improving performance.

- The winner knows to stay in the moment. One of my favorite lines from an unknown source is, "You don't have to run 26.2 miles; you have to run one mile 26 times, plus two tenths." There you go, it's that simple, said in jest, of course.

- The more efficient you become at getting in the zone during training runs will help you handle the marathon.

- Quitting must be an unacceptable outcome.

Please take note, those last two points are worth reading again and committing to memory.

A Marathon Legend Capsule

Unknown Legend

Gee, I wonder who this want-to-be is?

The year is 2033. In the making for years, the plan is about to come to fruition. Here is the deal. For too many years to count, this marathon runner has heard a dreaded question too often. Once and for all, he hopes to answer in the affirmative. The query, "Have you run the Boston Marathon?" If he's heard it once, it's been a thousand times.

He has always had to answer no, with a drooping face. You see, the Boston Marathon is the gold standard when it comes to marathons. Its' the world's oldest annual Marathon, going back to 1897, the year after the first Olympic Games one. It took the recent global pandemic to halt the race from being held, as it occurred during both World Wars.

Here's the thing. If you can't say yes to that query, one's Marathon's credibility is in short supply. So the next question is, "Why did it take until he was 80 years -old to do it?" A simple answer – his pace is too slow, period. You see, Boston is also a marathon one must qualify for, not like most, where one can enter by paying or getting in through the lottery. Not Boston. Here is why the year 2033 is in his sights. That year he turns 79 years old. The 80 – 84 age group's qualifying time goes to 4 hours and 50 minutes. If he stays in shape and keeps running, a big if, he believes, it will be doable. Wish me luck.

When I began running marathons at the age of 52, I naively thought I would have a shot at winning my age group at some point. But my cousin, a runner who has run Boston, which I jealously must add, informed me, "If people are running at an elder age, they are long-time runners, dedicated to it, and fast." Ah, I never thought of that, and it produces another "Oh well" moment.

As the saying goes, "Hope springs eternal," and that is what I cling to forever. I won't rule out the other option - working much harder to qualify before then, but I cringe thinking of giving more than I already do.

The last question, "Will I be satisfied if I never run the Boston Marathon?" Proud no matter what, but satisfied, unlikely.

My Story: Music for the Soul

Stood there boldly

Sweatin' in the sun

Felt like a million

Felt like number one...

I stood proud, I stood tall

High above it all

I still believed in my dreams

Bob Seger *"Like a Rock"*

Smile and Sing-Along

When the calendar turned to August in the baseball season, droopy eyes were unavoidable. After many months, the daily grind took its toll on the spirit and body. The fortunate players are those on teams in the running for post-season play. Those that weren't in the hunt were at a disadvantage because they lacked the added incentive. No matter, after thousands of swings, throws, hours, two more months of the same is the very definition of the dog days.

It doesn't take a rocket scientist to know that the fourth month of marathon training is the torrid one. I feel my ability to overcome the adversity of hours running comes from other times I had to dig deep. We've all had frustrating times, and my 1982 season with the Indians was an example. The season turned into a career disaster with nothing going right. I lost confidence, not that I had much anyway, and without it, I played scared. A well-deserved demotion came the next season, and there was no one to blame but me. I was faced with the reality of a difficult road back to the big leagues, if not an impossible one. Luckily, I came upon a solution — an above-normal focus, which bordered on obsession. It was a testament to what the mind can do, but it came with sacrifice, a price I was willing to pay.

My road back to the MLB is how an abundance of miles on foot feels — a challenge and sacrifice, but with the knowledge, finishing is possible if I can find the zone. I use the same passionate mentality I used to return to "The Show" for finishing the dog days phase of training.

Mind Games

It pays to be creative for getting through difficulty. One trick I use near the end of a strenuous run is my "smiling" playbook. Smiling alone can change one's attitude and is another perfect day ingredient. Even though it takes energy and commitment to do it, I grin at each passerby, of which there is no shortage of along Chicago's Lakefront. Because it's Chicago, 75% of people will not look at you, which adds to my already exhausted outlook. It's also no surprise, of those who look, a high percentage of the stranger's faces imply I must be a serial killer. But all is not lost. I bank on those few (out of towners, I suppose) who respond with a smile.

To get a smile or two or a slight wave is heavenly when one's energy is gone. You are probably like me with feeling recognition from another, notably with a smile, inspires as few things can. Often, I can picture their faces days later. Anthony J D'Angelo said, "Smile, it is the key that fits the lock of everybody's heart." Connie Stevens said, "Nothing you wear is more important than your smile." I concur with both assessments, as it lifts my spirits at a most needed juncture.

As you know by now, my most vital difference-maker to get in the zone is music. Songs help me understand life and provide self-reflection and motivation. A verse can bring me to a happy, thoughtful, and sentimental place and ignites creativity, peace, focus, and a needed distraction. Stirring words can put me in a meditative state, and health experts advocate mediation to no end, so it must be helpful.

I may not know until I get out on the trail what music I am in the mood for, and it varies from rap to easy listening. One may feel upbeat exercise music works best, but everyone's tastes vary. I prefer mellow tunes with meaningful words early and late in the run. I regularly need a pick me up in the middle, so I use songs that "kick it in." Whatever the genre, I am always on the lookout for verses I can use for contemplation and motivation. A song that speaks to me can make a mile or two zip by effortlessly.

Profound Incorporated

A top music inspiration comes from the music and story "Hamilton," the Broadway play. I speculate Lin-Manuel Miranda may have been writing his production with a

173

marathon in mind. I have listened to it in many marathons, and it always delivers to occupy my thoughts. The following verses inspire millions of other admirers and me:

"I'm willing to wait for it." **That line speaks to the patience to run long distances I never had years ago. Finishing is a fantastic achievement, and such a sense of accomplishment is worth the wait.**

"There's a million things I haven't done, just you wait." **A marathon will highlight those million, and it's the life philosophy to have.**

"I'm passionately smashin' every expectation. Every action's an act of creation!" **To prove to yourself and those who didn't think you could do something is creativity at its finest.**

"And when my time is up, have I done enough? Will they tell my story?" **It is hard to imagine anyone can do enough, but all I hope for is at least one person telling my story. My plot is to develop a narrative worth telling.**

"When you got skin in the game, you stay in the game." **At mile 15, you have skin and many other body parts in the game. The only choice is to stay in and finish.**

"And when our children tell our story, they'll tell the story of tonight." **Finishing a marathon defines you forever and beyond.**

"I will never be satisfied." **I know that will be true of my marathon finish time, but I hope it's the case in everything in life, too. Complacency leads to nowhere.**

13

The Patient Mindset

A Dream

I've been waiting for this moment for so long, and then, nothing? It's as if I'm in a cage, like an animal, and cannot wait to bust loose and roam again. The questions swirl, "Why are time, and I stuck when both should be flying by now? Will this waiting ever end?" My mind keeps pleading, "Let me out of here," but to no avail."

I wake in a sweat and reckon it's meaning. I realize this isn't only a dream; it is the last days and minutes before the marathon. I am so excited to compete, but the wait to begin is excruciating.

"Of all the hardships a person had to face, none was more punishing than the simple act of waiting."

Khaled Hosseini *"A Thousand Splendid Suns"*

As if another is needed, the waiting game is another challenge the competitor must overcome.

The success trail ends with, what else – winning. As stated in the beginning, being a winner is a state of mind, and that is what the two final stages involve.

Stairway to success:

25. Trust

26. Celebration

5th Month Training Steps – Winding Down

Lead Up to Race Day

A welcome feeling of relief comes once the dog days are behind you! Even though the preparation isn't over, you have survived the worst of it. Training schedules only have you run about 21 miles, so the monster runs are over. If you can do that amount, adrenaline on race day will bring you to the finish. The reasoning is solid for the most part, and traveling more miles would not give time for recovery before the race.

The pride in getting this far should be enormous, so be sure to **celebrate your health and self-discipline.** Recall you have accomplished what only the finest of athletes have. Another reason for the self-victory parade is you did it. What? Please take note of the schedule because it had you run 26 miles over two or three days. For example, the day before a 20-mile run, the program has me do 6 miles. Bingo! The two-day total is a confidence builder that you can finish the big one. Now, the simple task is to cover the whole distance in one day, I again joke.

Step twenty-five to success is trust - the belief you have given your all and that it will be enough to finish the goal. As with most things, one can look back and think they could have given more, but that sort of mind game helps nothing.

As written, with the marathon race day approaching fast, a gradual slowdown follows the highest workload. Instead of forty-plus mile weeks, the schedule eases each remaining week to only about 10 miles the week before. Doing less is surprisingly tricky because the competitor wants to keep pushing. The addiction to the daily workouts and many weekly miles makes doing less feel like you are settling for mediocrity.

Please understand rest is critical now. It's the time to restore and rebuild the mind and body. Even though it is customary to question whether you have done enough, you must trust the process. This easing is the time for the body to regain its power and the mind its enthusiasm. For practical use of your extra time, create a game plan and develop the race day mindset. Prime for that process is a continual, singular focus of planning to give your all.

An urgent tip in the last few weeks, which comes naturally in the virus age, is to shake hands with nobody. Even in past years, I warned friends not to take anything personal the weeks before the race. I would stop socializing and shaking hands the closer to the marathon. I discovered the hard way a sinus-cold before the race, although not a run killer, is annoying. The necessity of clear breathing should go without saying.

The game plan of extra rest, healthy fluids, and carbohydrates (pasta) the days before race day are musts, too. One should do online research for the most valuable foods to eat before a marathon. You will be grateful for doing it as the last marathon miles arrive.

One Week to Go

The first nerve-wracking day arrives with the seven-day weather forecast. I estimate it is pretty accurate about a week ahead for temperatures, wind, and humidity. A projection of ideal temperatures, light winds, and low humidity is the hope. It's a given that temperatures above 75 degrees, heavy rain, or high winds make the test more formidable. You will have some disappointment if those are the projection, but the good news is you have adequate time to prepare mentally. Of my fourteen marathons, only a couple had terrible weather, and those occurred in Las Vegas, a most unlikely spot. **Once again, the athlete in you understands perfect conditions are rare as your mindset by now is, "Bring it on."**

Like looking forward to a family reunion or vacation, the anticipation builds the closer race day gets. With each passing day, the body and mind are in a frenzy to get out and run again. That disposition is what you want. I was exceedingly "itching to go" by marathon day for each of my marathons.

It's hard to get your thoughts off the race the week before, and you may notice the mind wandering more at work and home. Another drawback that may come is the usual fear and nervousness, which come with beginnings. A big difference from the baseball start is a marathon is one day, the winner takes all. Marathon redemption the next day, week, or month doesn't exist for most runners. A long recovery period is needed, more than for most sports. **A marathon has the pressure of everything riding on the day's performance, and failing to finish means a long offseason. On the plus side, the anticipation of "gameday" is palpable in your attitude, with a lighter step as many friends ask if you are ready.**

In the last week, it's beneficial to begin to write the must-haves for race day. These early calculations give you time to add to it as the race nears. The last thing you want is to get to the race and realize you forgot a prime item. For example, I arrived at the starting area in my first marathon with my numbered bib unattached to my shirt, a peril of being a rookie and overexcited. Without it visible, one gets yanked off the course. One way or the other, I am going, but it would be uncomfortable to run 26 miles having to hold it out front the whole way. As you can imagine, finding safety pins at 5:45 AM was almost as great an ordeal as trekking the four-plus hours. Divine assistance came through in the nick of time by way of a hotel clerk.

The Day Before

It's surprising how many little things there are to prepare the day before. Early in the day, set aside the items listed on your race day must-haves so you can relax a little. Other 'to-do's" include a plan for getting to the race and meeting with friends after. Races close many streets, so a calculated plot for getting there on time takes work. For the well-attended races, you should get there an hour or two before the race. A post-marathon meeting place is a must. Often, non-runners cannot get into the finish area, and you will want attending friends' support upon finishing, as your physical condition may demand some help.

From my experience and as implied, do not expect to sleep well the night before. Many reflections swirl around once your head hits the pillow. The insecurity of knowing if you will have enough to finish will haunt you the most. Instead of getting perturbed about insomnia, **use the sleepless time to visualize the fun you will have, which I say half-jokingly.**

Step twenty-six — taking the time to swell in self-pride. Even though winning the race is not in the cards, you are a winner by getting to the starting line and creating an identity to be proud of forever. The fantastic achievement required courage, sacrifice, and regularly tested dedication. **Relish the moment because you have done something "average" cannot do**. For the final motivation, consider your reasons for doing what you have done and take comfort in knowing you are a better you. As you rejoice, remember there are rarely times for the opportunity to become A Hero.

One last tip is necessary – prepare to "bring your Cool." Remember, the amount of organization that goes into putting a marathon on is mind-boggling. Like during the race, a good chance the unexpected shows up before it, so prepare to have patience with the volunteers who are there to help because theirs may be in short supply.

Finally, the wait is over. Tomorrow is a day at least five months in waiting!

A Marathon Legend Capsule

Impossible? Not so fast, just Incredibly Fast

A winner sets out to be the best physically and mentally.

To put the following feat in perspective, imagine having to drive a little over 26 miles, but in horrendous, big-city traffic. A friend left simultaneously as you on foot. Upon arriving, the runner is having a water bottle when you arrive.

In the year I was born, 1954, Roger Bannister was the first to run a mile in under four minutes. Many people thought it never could be done, but many others have done it since Roger. Bannister's breakthrough proved that once others realize it's possible, the impossible isn't that anymore.

In 2019, in a unique, not open event, Kenyan Eliud Kipchoge ran a sub-2-hour marathon. It seems inhuman, but with the mental hurdle not there anymore, someone doing it in an actual marathon may not be far off. There is a fantastic chance the current world record holder, the same guy, Eliud Kipchoge, will be the one to do it. He doesn't have too far to go because his current world record is 2:01.39.

Like many elite marathon runners, Eliud was world-class in the 3- and 5-thousand-meter events before jumping into marathon running. The speed was there already. Here's the thing, to run under two hours, one must be under five-minute miles for 26.2 miles. That is mind-blowing and flying data. Another impressive aspect of Eliud is that many articles are about his philosophical quotes. It's apparent he embraces being a role model and preaches the power of discipline to reach one's potential.

Here are a few examples followed by my take:

"Self-discipline starts with you. It's no other person. It starts with you. Start to examine yourself...Self discipline is doing what's right instead of doing what you feel like doing. That's the meaning of self-discipline." **I love this one because it gets back to being accountable for one's direction and effort.**

'Pleasure in what you're doing puts perfection in your work. In any profession, you should think positively. That's the driver of your mind. If your mind is thinking positive thoughts, you are on the right track. **So insightful, and it is my life and coaching philosophy to a T.**

"Personally, I believe in what I am doing. To run a big marathon and win, it takes five months. When I am on the starting line, my mind starts to think of what I have been doing for the last five months. I believe in my training. I treat myself as the best one on that line because my mind is telling me that I am the best, and I believe in what I am doing in the last five months. I can run free. I can run free, and that's what actually has helped me to be successful." **As I wrote before, few things are better than freedom, as he also implies.**

Indeed, a guy worth admiring for more than his athletic feats. Good luck, Eliud; get that sub-2-hour mile as I work to stay under five hours.

My Story: Getting Pumped

"You can go the distance

You can run the mile

You can walk straight through hell with a smile

You can be the hero You can get the gold

Breaking all the records

they thought never could be broke

Yeah, do it for your people

Do it for your pride

How are you ever gonna know

if you never even try?"

The Script *"Hall of Fame "*

Peaceful Opening Days

My vast baseball experience gives me the most significant boost on race day because the last weeks of marathon training are the same as the days before baseball's opening day. As spring training wound down, the excitement for the coming season would grow each day. I prepared with positive meditations and seeing myself performing well in front of crowds. My state of mind was one of determination and excitement; knowing the chance to put the hard work to the test was near. A natural hesitance came with the challenge ahead, but it's time to embrace a long-cherished dream.

An encouraging sign is Baseball's Opening Day was the day I felt the least nervous. I had the confidence and peace I never had for the season's remainder. The calm helped me have many productive first days.

Also, my playoff experiences are a big help on race day. To that point, in 1980, I played in three of the last four games in the 1980 season when our Dodger team had to beat the Houston Astros to make the playoffs. The games were of the direst but exciting variety — "win or go home." We almost pulled off the feat until losing on the fourth day. Other similar pressure-packed playoffs in minor league baseball help me realize I could rise to the occasion. Those situations helped develop a "fearless" attitude for each marathon. Of course, I've never competed without nervous tension, but the athletic mindset of courage is critical to be ready for what's to come.

My Race Day Prep

I treat marathon day as a playoff game. It is not only an event to look forward to, but I view it as a reward for the hard work. Sure, sleepless nights before big moments come with the territory, but it's a small price to pay. Before a competition, I have gratitude for the opportunity to do something I love. For the days leading up to race day, I feel like a prime-time athlete again. With my visualization now at its peak, I see myself out on the course and kicking butt. Well, at least on the course. It's "Glory-days-time!"

To keep the tension at bay and prepare, I watch inspirational sports movies the days before. My favorites include Miracle, Rocky, Chariots of Fire, and Remember the Titans. I also find stories about underdogs' overcoming unbelievable circumstances and review the book "Born to Run" with its many compelling characters.

And it's natural to recall some trite and corny motivational phrases I have heard since young, like:

* "It's time to walk the talk." **In other words, run with attitude.**

* "When the going gets tough, the tough get going." **Ah yes, mental toughness is what I plan to be all about.**

* Win one for the Gipper." **I'm dating myself with this one, but I want to win for others, too.**

"Where there is a will, there is a way." **Where there is a finish line, I will find it.**

* "Ready or not, here I come!" **Search, and you will find a way.**

* "Never quit." **To the point, not always possible, but the demeanor to have.**

I also search for motivational running quotes. Some of my favorites are humorous and useful to ease the tension. Which reminds me, **Laughter is another ingredient that goes into a perfect day.** *Some of these you notice in fan* *signs during the marathon. As usual, I give my analysis after.*

"All it takes is all you got." **Marc Davis – That doesn't seem to be too much to ask?**

"May the course be with you." **A movie-worthy line if there ever was one!**

"Whether you think you can or think you can't, you're right." **Henry Ford – That's a truthful twist.**

"Life is either a daring adventure or nothing." **Helen Keller – Another life choice that should be obvious but not always taken.**

"Fake it til you make it." **There lies my marathon plan!**

Finally, I sing The Impossible Dream in the shower before going to bed, "To run where the brave dare not go" **That line says it all and excites me to no end.**

14
The Hero's Mindset

A Dream

What an incredible feeling. I hit one out of the park. I touch first base with enormous pride. I cruise to second, and the joy is overwhelming. Ah, the sweet smell of success as I approach and race around third base. It's heading for home when trouble looms. What? No home plate. OK, let me circle again, the same result, over and over, trapped in an eternal cycle. Please, where's the end?

Another cruel nightmare, but the meaning is obvious – it's the sensation one has in a marathon of a never-ending road.

"I'm not telling you it's going to be easy... I'm telling you it's going to be worth it."

Art Williams – Motivational author

If you want to know what a marathon is like, those lines encapsulate the experience — a day of toil and ecstasy.

The success trail entails combining everything one has learned in practice – the mental and physical – to give their best when it counts the most — on game day.

Stairway to success:

Hero!

The Marathon – Race Day

Apply the Steps to "Bring it Home"

You have put in a remarkable amount of work and are so close to accomplishing a hearty goal, if not a lifelong dream. The encouraging news is that you have set the stage for high achievement by getting to the starting line. To say one is excited at this juncture is an understatement. The only thing in your way, implied throughout this book, is dreams do not come easily, and you must go the whole way to get to hero status. Let me warn you; this chapter mimics a marathon – it is long and tedious. Suffice it to say, you will need every physical step and the 26.2 "runner, athlete, winner, and hero" steps to weave it all together and cross the finish line. Of comfort is knowing you have the plan to succeed; it's just a matter of following it.

I will not say which step is most important because leaving any out can be the death blow to one's goal. Furthermore, each one is a building block to the blueprint you need to complete the task at hand. Before taking off, it's time to review the foundation steps.

Stairway to Heaven

Step 1 is finding a goal. By now, you know you have taken on one of the most challenging goals - running 26.2 miles. My baseball career taught me how to accomplish a daunting task by making it an extension of my being. That process is how I approach running and what you must do, knowing committing to such a level is the way to complete the most prominent examinations.

Step 2 is having the courage to try. One could say daring is central to a life well-lived. The things to know are:

- Dreams stay that way until you go for them.

- It takes guts to try, especially knowing failure is possible, if not likely.

- Life is boring without heading out that door.

- The definition of courage. Dictionary.com says it is "The quality of mind or spirit that enables a person to face difficulty, danger, pain without fear." The marathon will present the first three, and the bravery part is on you.

Step 3 is gathering the knowledge needed to give yourself the highest chance to succeed. The assembling in this instance was your five months of strenuous training. The observations along the way provided critical information for race day. You came to know the importance of the temperatures at the start, middle, and finish, along with awareness of any precipitation, wind, and uphill stretches. You realize educated decisions on food, fluids, and clothing are predominant on the big day. As hard as it is to admit, even with vast experience, I messed many things up in my athletic endeavors, which deterred my enjoyment of them.

Step 4 is knowing failure doesn't diminish you when you give your all. It's good to recall not everyone can be the winner. The good news is you have changed for the better because of the necessary, exceptional discipline and dedication. You've won, no matter the outcome, because of the:

- Improved self-confidence

- Healthier lifestyle

- Positive life outlook

Step 5 is the motivation – the establishment of a dynamic why. I know firsthand of the fantastic feelings one gets from pledging to something beyond "me." You came to understand that an others-oriented purpose gives more joy and incentive than focus only on oneself." Remember, the more committed you are to an external cause, the more likely you will persevere the challenging roads ahead.

Step 6 is having an accountability map. No mystery exists for that in marathon training. One either followed the mileage schedule and remained healthy or not. Gameday accountability is "another animal" and will come from accepting all the race challenges and the dedication to doing your best.

Steps 7 and 8 is the critical execution phase — a strategy and routine. Neglect of details can be costly, and the top athletes take nothing for granted. Stress is inescapable, but a review of your game plan and attention to every detail enables you to accept the tension. The resulting focus and feeling of preparedness help with a relaxed mind, which eases the pressure.

Step 9 is knowing one's limitations. You've learned race and game day are when to push beyond normal, but boundaries still exist. Finishing with your personal best time is always a desire, but the primary goal is to make it to the finish line. The key is staying tuned into the body and mind and not doing anything that risks long-term health.

Psyche Up in the Starting Area

Getting ready mentally for each long training trek may have been difficult, but a "Sky High" feeling will take care of itself on marathon day. The pent-up nervousness builds adrenaline, which athletes use to energize and overcome. **Remember, this is the World Series for runners.**

But before taking off, and as if the thought of 26.2 miles is not heavy enough, one must idle away the time in the starting area. In the big marathons, thousands of runners are waiting with you to get to the starting line, and it takes time to get there. Like Christmas morning and having to wait for your parents' permission to open presents, the minutes seem like hours. Also, don't be surprised if your legs feel exhausted from standing around, but know they are not.

To keep the tension at bay, small talk with others can help. It is fun to find out about strangers' past marathon history and compare stories. I am generally in such a mental zone I keep that to a minimum and have the mindset of before big games in my playing career. **I sense the pressure, and the excitement of knowing it's all on me now creates a unique focus.**

Step 10 is applying the health and safety measures. The good news is the marathon has a marked course, so your attention can go towards hydration and eating tips. While waiting, I set my plan of eating and drinking everything offered along the marathon course to avoid crashing out later. Other initial checks include correctly tied shoes, stretched legs, and ready listening material.

Enjoy the Thrill Miles: 1 – 7

Step 11 is putting in the work, knowing corner-cutting will not cut it. At last, the moment you have been gearing towards for the past half-year is here. When you cross the starting line, scream, or at the least, give a thumbs up to celebrate the kick-off. Your workday begins, and payday is around the next bend, or two, or twenty. History tells you the path to the finish line exists only by applying extraordinary effort.

Step 12 is **staying in the moment through discipline and patience.** Against all inclination, it is strategic not to force the action. You sense you could win a hundred-yard dash at the start, but don't forget, that is not what a marathon is. A trap is going out too fast and spending the energy you will need later. It's urgent to maintain control early, so you will have what it takes later, so be sure to

192

watch your pace, especially those out for a specific finish time. It's hard not to wish it to be over when the difficulty comes, but the key is to take in the atmosphere. It's vital to focus on the mile you are in and not worry about the future miles.

Step 13 is having a heightened sense of excitement and optimism. You may say, "Duh," that's obvious. But although a given at the start, maintaining an enthusiastic demeanor is not as easy as you think. I like to give myself an early pep talk that goes like this: "**I know I can succeed on any given day and today is that day. I will keep negative thoughts away and trust things will work out with tunnel vision to the finish line.**"

Settle into the Cruising Miles: 8 – 13

Step 14 is avoiding overconfidence. In every one of my marathons, after ten miles, I've said, "I feel great," and "Today I will run my personal best." Trouble looms the minute you let your guard down, so keep the swagger in check. Please note the following, the race's most challenging phase has not made its appearance yet, and **once an athlete assumes it's easy to win, sports have a way of dissuading the sentiment.**

Step 15 is a natural follow-up - understanding sports' unpredictable nature that each day is distinct and presents a new challenge. Here's the thing, you will not know until out on the course how the body and mind will respond. The secret is to accept the situations you face and make the best of them. Do not forget you are a fine-tuned machine, and success never comes without a fight.

Expect the Self-doubt: Miles 14 – 19

Step 16 is overcoming when the self-doubt arrives. As the race miles pile up, practice experience plays a more significant role as "the teacher" for what's about to follow. After the half marathon is when things get interesting, I chuckle because demanding, if not overwhelming, might be more appropriate designations. Another severe obstacle tends to show after the halfway point - uncertainty. As the early excitement and miles dissipate, the awful truth of what you got yourself into hits. Yep, you are only halfway there, and each mile seems to get further. Unless it's a great day, the dreaded idea of "Maybe it's OK to walk a little" may come. Do all you can to resist the urge to stroll because giving in will justify it for the remainder, leading to dissatisfaction.

Step 17 is embracing the identity of who you are. One solution for staying committed is living up to who you want to be. **In this case, you are a runner, athlete, and winner, and t**hat development alone is a significant accomplishment that brings with it pride. Realize this: many people never make moves to change who they are, and that is not you. **Your new character provokes the competitive spirit of never settling for less.**

Persevere the Dog Days: Miles 20 -23

Step 18 is the means to finish, which says a lot — the mind's ability to influence your direction. How important is this maneuver? **The remaining steps are all about the mental game, which attests to the significance of sports' cerebral nature.** By now, you know a marathon is an exercise in energy depletion, time consumption, and seemingly unending miles. The physical and mental grind test your psychological and physical strength to their core. So, it bears repeating; **never underestimate what the mind can accomplish. Your mental outlook will be the difference.**

The mental game with distance running is unique because you can do it while focusing on the unrelated. Most sports require concentration on an object or skill. With running, you can divert the mind and keep moving. Thinking of anything but running may be a good thing and your ace in the hole when pain and boredom come is daydreaming. The mind wanderings can help set the miles into cruise control as much as possible. Know that each mile completed without thought of each agonizing step keeps away the inclination to walk or stop. Of course, a previous lesson of safety must always come first, but if you must walk at some point, do it, just keep moving.

Now is also the time to use any mental tricks gathered from the months of training. If you planned well, you have a few self-pep-talks ready. Another helpful strategy is to count down the miles. As you see mile marker 20, thinking six instead of 26.2 is somewhat comforting, if not motivational. Another trick is saving your most inspirational material for now. For example, your favorite music or a super-interesting podcast can help at this time. I had a big ace in the hole for one marathon with my daughter's upcoming wedding speech to prepare. I saved the task until mile 21, and rehearsing it made the last few miles move by with only minor trauma.

Continue to Engage the Mental Game Absolutes

Step 19 is kicking adversity's tail. After knowing hardship will come and preparing for it, one must go about defeating it. Perhaps, nothing defines you as a winner more than this action. The ending miles try you as few other things do. It helps to look at what the top athletes do, again. They use self-doubt and embrace uneasiness for motivation, knowing a reorientation of attitude is possible. It may help to evoke the people who questioned you had what it takes to do this. That recollection is an excellent motivator because you know you cannot live with the hurt of telling them you did not finish. The notion of having to admit defeat can provide incentive. Reservations brought on by self and others can sustain you when most needed.

Step 20 is to enjoy the crusade. It's easy to have a lack of fun when an incredible amount of focus, work, and pain is necessary, but dreading it defeats the purpose of doing something. Even in these most difficult times, **remember, it's why you play — the struggle, attention, and intention make it worthwhile.** Be sure to take in the sights and sounds, as they help divert the mind from the mentioned obstacles. Acknowledging the fans' vitality and celebrating each passed mile marker also help with keeping momentum. **A fantastic way to keep it fun is to implement the essentials that go into a perfect day - a smile, gratitude, prayer, laughter, sharing, singing, meditation, and loving.**

Step 21 is a critical factor to perseverance — adaptation. If it is up to the body alone at this stage, you will stop, or at the least, walk it in. When the athlete stays attentive to what's going on, they can make the changes to keep on track, and those begin with mind manipulation.

You will see a mile marker in the distance and swear it has been at least two or three since the last designation. "No," it has only been one. "Dang," you want to swear, but you do not have the extra energy to waste. The whole body begins to feel the pain, and it starts to affect the mind, but shaping your thoughts keeps you astride. Bear in mind, every time an athlete competes, they have the choice of quitting or sticking to it. It helps to think of the athletic concepts you have heard since young that speak to perseverance:

"Work when others aren't."

"There is no such thing as can't."

"Winners never quit, and quitters never win." A Vince Lombardi quote which once again dates me.

Climb Over-the-Wall — Miles 23 – 26.2

The worst miles, at least mentally, are behind you because knowing the nearby finish line takes some of the anxiety away. You are so close now you can taste it, and that sense is motivation itself. However, you will have to get over the wall to get there. At this juncture, the body and mind tighten like trying to accelerate with the brake pedal pressed. It's the dreaded "wall" – when everything about you says you have nothing left. Although it may seem the highest barrier you have ever seen, you have come too far not to climb it. Although your pace is probably just beyond a fast walk now, **summon the marathon runner's code, not finishing is not an option**, and repeat to yourself, "I got this."

197

You are so close to the 1% territory of athletic achievement, so take comfort in that and the fact you are an elite athlete. Additionally, you are a winner because only they have this competitiveness and conditioning level. Now, it's on to become a hero. Every ounce of competitive spirit is a priority now, and if you are a prayer person, now is the time for it.

Step 22 is finding the zone. The winner has an increased ability to focus when things get most daunting. In a marathon, they divert their thoughts from the physical and mental pain. Additionally, they visualize achieving what they set out to and keep faith in themselves. **Concentration is always the athlete's ace in the hole.**

Step 23 is essential before, initially, and throughout — acclimating to the conditions. The playing conditions on marathon day usually involve the weather and the uphill climbs. One can prepare for the slopes in training, but the weather on a designated day is a variable. For example, my son's first marathon was in Edinburg, Scotland, and the temperatures were an uncharacteristic mid 80's range. Another instance one cannot plan for was my friend's daughter, who ran the 2018 Boston Marathon. What a thrill for her, only to have driving winds in a cold downpour the entire race. If you wondered why this step is in the mental adjustment phase, these examples recognize why acclimating is psychological. Mind control is everything when conditions are out of the ordinary.

In well-attended marathon events, a common situation is congestion from a high number of entrants. You must be ready with good vision to dodge the slower runners and those who dart around. Keen eyes and feet help keep one safe until the crowding ends. You may have to veer right, left, and through to remain upright. The most practical advice I can give you is to stay on a direct path as best you can. Failing to do so can mean traveling much more than 26.2 miles. As other situations arise, and they will, one must be ready to adjust. The right call on food, fluids, and clothing is paramount to finishing, too. Remember, distance running's opponents are the miles, weather, track, and one's inner being.

Earn Your Pay Off – The Hero Line

Step 24 is another invaluable move necessary at this juncture — trust in your spirit and training. By mile 21, complete reliance on your commitment, dedication, and desire is of utmost importance. Another self-pep talk may help, although its effectiveness now is dubious. It's worth a try, so here goes. **"I trust the months of practice were for this moment. I must push beyond what I thought possible and realize my potential. I will not accept "average" because it creates a regret I choose not to have. I believe in me!"**

You know from your workouts that a gut check will arrive, and it's crucial to recognize you overcame it repeatedly. Not only is trust in one's preparation necessary, but a belief in your reasons for doing this from the beginning is also helpful. Eliciting your initial, profound "why" to run a marathon provides the strength. For me, I think of the Kids of St. Jude's Hospital and realize any pain is trivial in comparison. I recall the people who donated to my cause and thank them. After these introspections, my steps seem a bit lighter.

Step 25 is closing it out with the final push. Talk about a sight for sore eyes, sore body, painful everything. Spotting the finish line may bring tears of joy because the end is the culmination of a dream, not to mention the work. However, it is no time to take your eyes off the prize. Even though the finish line is within sight, many things can go wrong. I found out many times in my career, "It ain't over till it's over." Yogi Berra again, but it's true that you should not celebrate until crossing the line. Many a team and player let their guard down before the end line, and success slipped away. After this long on the course, it's not uncommon to see runners keeled over and unable to move even though they are so close to the end.

Webster defines hero with the terms "legendary figure" and "illustrious warrior." It further defines it as a person admired by others for noble qualities and great courage. After reading those, I believe there are few monikers better than "Hero." Knowing that is what awaits you at the finish line makes the last mile seem not so bad. To become one is the final motivation needed to complete the job. The crossing means being able to say for the rest of your life, "I have run a marathon," which makes it all worth it.

Step 26 is celebrating your hard-earned status. There are few sports feelings as satisfying as finishing a marathon. Of course, with zero energy to emote, only a wry smile may come, but the sense of accomplishment is world-class, knowing it is a feat few have done. You were probably not, or ever sure, you would do it, but you are now in the "Superstar" category of athletes. Perhaps the highlight is getting to the end helps you forget the many instances you said, "Why the "ef" did I put myself through this?" and the times you walked, swore, and pledged never to do this again. **The relief is overwhelming and helps take the negative concepts away.** The pain you may be in can make the forgetting temporary but acknowledge you are a Hero! Any time one can pull off the improbable, if not seemingly impossible, the designation is applicable. *You just won the World Series of running, and your marathon finishers' medal is lifelong proof of your greatness.*

It's worth reiterating, not everyone will finish, but that is no reason to hang your head. If you can say, "I gave my all and left everything out there," you won. Rejoice, take solace, and **use the temporary failure as motivation to try again, a decision that also confirms your winner's identity.** Remember, giving your all is enough to be satisfied, pride-filled, and victorious — period.

A Marathon Legend Capsule

Big Things in Small Packages

No barrier was too significant for this remarkable athlete.

One saying I've always loved, partly because it applies to me in my sport of baseball, is, "It's not how big you are; it's how big you play." That quip sums up 5-foot 2-inch, 100-pound Joan Benoit Samuelson. I feel other connections to this incredible marathon runner, too. In 1979, I wore the Blue of the Los Angeles Dodgers, while Joan Benoit won the Boston Marathon sporting a Boston Red Sox cap – so cool, and she was a relatively unknown marathoner at the time. She would not remain that way, as she went on to set Marathon records in Boston and Chicago that held for many years later, a sure sign of greatness.

Speaking of Los Angeles, in 1984, she won the Gold Medal in the first women's Olympic marathon. I read and reread that so many times, thinking 1984 could not have been the first women's Marathon, but true. I relate to Joan the most, though, because she is an American Grand Masters marathon champion, which means the elderly, like me. At age 50, she competed in the Olympic Team trials and ran a 2:49 marathon. And she has continued to set records for runners in their fifties. In 2019, forty years after her win in the Boston Marathon, she competed again and ran it in 3:04. "Are you kidding me, not even in my dreams?"

I mentioned earlier that it's essential to reach for dreams, but also vital is the sharing of what one learns to help others. Again, Joan Benoit Samuelson passes that test with writing books and motivational speaking. Additionally, she adheres to my advice of continuing to look for goals to achieve and the "move it or lose it" philosophy. In summary, talk about someone "Born to Run."

My Story: Show Time

Every night I lie in bed

The brightest colors fill my head

A million dreams are keeping me awake

I think of what the world could be

A vision of the one I see

A million dreams is all it's gonna take

A million dreams for the world we're gonna make

The Greatest Showman *"A Million Dreams"*

Day of Days

Many thoughts come in the marathon, and for me, many bring back memories of competing in the majors. For example, you would not have trouble spotting the starting pitcher for the day's game. Why? He is the one with the Game Face — a severe blank stare, unaware of anything around them. Their attention is already in the game, facing batters. That personality is me the hours before the race. I am there physically, greet, and respond to people, but my mind is 26.2 miles away. It's like giving a presentation in front of a large crowd, and your mind is in an ultimate focus mode. Your demeanor changes from everyday experiences, and the intense focus is apparent.

At the starting line, a cautious excitement persists. The pressure is thrilling and nerve-wracking at the same time.

I am no longer playing second base, one of nine defenders on the ballfield. I am now the starting pitcher, the central attraction. The ball is in my hands, and it's time for the ultra-competitor to come forth.

Safety First, and Always, But?

Before every marathon I have run, caution comes from the movie A Few Good Men. In one scene, Demi Moore's character knows Tom Cruise may have to put it all on the line and risk his career. She warns him it may not be worth it to keep going, "Listen when you're up there today if you feel like it's not going to happen," and he gets the point. I go into the race, knowing I will put it all on the line. Yet, I understand it's OK to back off and live for another time if I don't have it. At the same time, I believe I have no reason not to "have it" today. Therein lies the dichotomy of the competitor's personality — to play with a never-give-up stance with the understanding it's not worth risking one's future either.

The Thrill of Competing Again

As alluded to earlier, the calm and quiet confidence that came on baseball's opening day works on race day. The day before my races, the nerves are sky high, and resting does not come easily. But, upon waking on race day, I feel serene. I am comfortable and excited to have the center stage again in front of thousands of fans. It's like I am up to bat again. Into my mind pops the movie For Love of the Game with Kevin Costner saying, "Clear the mechanism," as he tunes out the noise. I know to eliminate my mind's negative-chatter and the pressure associated with the competition.

Game Day Execution

My career taught me it's one thing to have a blueprint, but implementing it is the secret to victory. Winners execute, and that is my disposition from the beginning. My strategy is simple and comes from Walt Stack, who said, "Start slow, then taper." Bingo! That is my philosophy in a nutshell. I know going out too fast will leave less, or no, fight in the end. A line from the book Born to Run helps me, "If you have a choice between one step or two between rocks, take three." The three-step hint always seems to help me find a comfortable pace.

Optimism Rules

I played baseball with little confidence at the big-league level, but I always had optimism things would work out if I continued to grind away. I have the same rosy outlook in the marathon with faith in me and the training. I call to mind Kurt Russell's speech as Herb Brooks in Miracle. "Great moments are born from great opportunity... This is your time. Now go out there and take it." Thanks, Kurt and Coach Brooks, that provides the inspiration to do this.

Taking in the Moment

Added excitement comes with friends and family members in attendance. I think of John Travolta in the movie Grease. He has perfect form, speed, and confidence to impress when the girl (Olivia Newton-John) shows up. I ask friends and family to let me know where they will be watching so I know where to stride like a gazelle. Athletes must show confidence, so the opposition doesn't know it may be getting the best of them.

206

Another source of enjoyment comes from reading the many signs along the route. Many have creativity, wit, and an ability to make one smile, which helps in the treacherous miles.

Here are some of my favorites, followed by my rationalizations:

- *Go Mike and below in parentheses (only Mike).* **Hey, what about me?**

- *Worst parade ever.* **I concur.**

- *Race day isn't the challenging part; it is the reward.* **I'm sure that wise guy has never run one.**

- *If you feel good when running a marathon, don't worry, you will get over it.* **The most valid statement ever made.**

- *That awkward moment when you are wearing Nike, and you just can't do it.* **I have been there many times.**

- *It sounded like a good idea four months ago.* **So many smart alecks in the world today.**

- *You have great endurance; call me.* **Easy to remember that one.**

- *Naked cheerleaders next mile.* **Another unforgettable one.**

- *The Kenyans are already done.* **Rub it in while you're at it.**

- *Whine now, wine later.* **Finally, one that makes perfect sense.**

Preparing for Murphy

Each of my 14 marathons has gone differently, and I realize it's why they play the games. Murphy's Law is something will go wrong, and it is almost a given while exercising for hours. I believe he must have been scurrying far when he arrived at his Law. Of course, some events go wrong before even getting to the starting line. One year, on a ride to the marathon, the closest we could get was a mile from the starting gun. Great! The dread of having to run a mile to be on time before even starting was disheartening and embarrassing. It was a reminder not to panic or forget the enemy, Murphy. I summon up the movie The Natural, and in the biggest at-bat of his life, Roy Hobbs (Robert Redford) breaks his immortal bat – "Wonderboy." There is no panic as he tells the bat boy to pick out a winner, and the youngster returns with "Savoy Special," which performs flawlessly.

Enduring the Dog Days

The most intimidating miles, the dog days, are from mile 15 until about the 23-mile marker. Of course, the entire ending miles are precarious, but knowing the finish line is near takes the edge away the last few miles. To aid in this section, I recall one of my biggest thrills in the Major Leagues. As a Chicago White Sox, I wore number 42, Jackie Robinson's number, which is now retired by every team. I, too, played second base for The Los Angeles Dodgers, another connection to the great man. The last miles' difficulty is nothing compared to what Jackie endured and had to overcome. Memories of those who overcame harsh conditions help one through unpleasant times, and I do my best to channel Jackie Robinson's intense focus to reach the end. Centering one's thoughts minimize obstacles and pain.

Living Up to Your Identity

A line in my favorite movie, Chariots of Fire, comes to me with the end almost a reality. Harold Abrahams says, "10 lonely seconds to justify my whole existence." A little dramatic, but it is how I feel about finishing. Unfortunately, it is more than 10 seconds, about 40 minutes, but finishing justifies who I want to be – a hero, at least to me. With such a prize afoot, I will do everything in my power to complete the task at hand.

Facing Reality

Every race, I've intended a mad dash to the finish line. But reality wins out. The mind and body are both shouting now, "This is it, my last marathon; I will never do one again." I accept the sentiment and say, "No, not a sprint in me today," It's OK, finishing was the objective, and I did my best even as my mind wanders to the winners.

The elite pack of runners has run 26.2 miles, showered, had lunch, watched a movie, and I am still on the course. That isn't a comforting thought, but I know finishing creates the same satisfaction as winning does for them. Of course, if you tell me the marathon winner can steal a base as I could in the MLB, I quit. I check my finish time and wince a little, as it, as always, seems slower than the one wished to have. Maybe next time, I will do better, but that's sports and life's reality in the slow lane.

Game Hero

Upon finishing, pride seizes the moment. I imagine hearing Lou Gehrig in "Pride of the Yankees." Ravaged by cancer, he says, "Yet today I consider myself the luckiest man on the face of the earth." I always cry thinking of that moment and relate to the words in a much-less dire situation, of course. I hang my finisher medals alongside my World Series Trophy, and they bring equal pride to being a member of the 1981 World Champion Los Angeles Dodgers.

15
The Analytical Mindset

A Dream

I keep missing a routine ground ball, and I hit the same pothole time and again, even though I know it's there. I've made this play thousands of times in my life and have taken millions of steps without issue. What is going on?

And I wake. This nightmare is like my first one – it's the result of a lifetime of baseball and running. The mind is in a state of analysis, awake and asleep, for the good and the bad, and is the athlete's constant companion.

"Always the student, the learner. Never the expert."

Allistair McCaw

Well said, and critical advice to follow.

You may have thought the finish line was the end of the success trail, but a couple more ingredients are necessary.

Stairway to success:

26.1. Analysis

26.2 Summary

Recap, Rewind, Re-plan

I know I promised 26.2 steps to success, and I have not forgotten that pledge.

Step 26.1 — an honest analysis of performance. As evidenced by my earlier New York Marathon review, the lessons and learning do not stop at the race's end. Even though fulfillment from finishing exists, the athlete always asks, "Why didn't I do better?" Figuring out the plusses and minuses from an attempt helps move on and be better prepared for the future.

After every game in my playing career, it didn't take long to wonder what went wrong. I know I prepared and gave what I had, but the competitor's curse takes over - believing better is always possible. The fighter is never satisfied, and why they over-work, over-think, and over-try to gain an edge — win, lose, or draw, the work to improve continues.

Even though one may have solid reasons for underperforming, excuses and negativity diminish the effort. When answers to "why" come, it is valuable to frame them in ways that make you feel like you overcame them. Instead of saying, "The weather slowed my time," I say, "I battled some horrible conditions and made it." Instead of, "Cramps kept me from the time I hoped for," it is, "I learned today I must hydrate better to prevent cramps." **Winners analyze in a positive tone.**

Step 26.2 sums the success trail process up —
consistency and conviction. What did it take to achieve?
It took uniformity of movement, training, and attitude to
get to the finish line — one physical and psychological
step followed by another. Finally, as mentioned many
times, **winning will only prove possible with the**
conviction of purpose. Most attempts fail because of a
lack of a deeply felt "why." Whenever players and teams
are not "All in," failure follows, and regrets come soon
when one realizes they left a lot on the table.

A Marathon Legend Capsule

Teamwork

I haven't left out many sports cliches in this book, so I would be remiss not to use one of the most circulated ones, "There is no I in team." The following story personifies the phrase to the utmost, along with the very definition of Hero.

I began the capsules with a story that had me crying, so ending on one with waterfalls seems appropriate. You will not hear their names when people consider the greatest athletes ever, but perhaps, they should be. It's hard to know where to start when talking about Dick and Rick Hoyt. They are in the Ironman Hall of Fame, and a statue of them sits near the start of the Boston Marathon. You may not have recognized their names individually, but the *Team Hoyt* name is more known.

Rick Hoyt was born with Cerebral Palsy, but that didn't deter him from getting a degree in special education from Boston University. After, he worked there on developing systems to help people with disabilities. Rick, who has quadriplegia, would communicate by typing through a computer, and after the first time his dad pushed him in a wheelchair, he said, "Dad, when I'm running, it feels like I'm not disabled."

So, how did his dad, Dick Hoyt, a retired Lieutenant Colonel in the Air National Guard, respond to that. Although not a runner before that, he arguably became one of the greatest athletes by pushing his son in over a thousand races, including 72 marathons and 257 triathlons. It was always about "team" with them and inspiring others to believe in the beauty of family, sport, and determination. ESPN honored the pair with its perseverance award in 2013, and their pictures may eventually be next to the word in the dictionary someday, I jest. Dick Hoyt passed away in 2021, but his legacy of family, fatherhood, and teamwork will live forever.

I would say that team Hoyt exemplifies every one of the 26.2 steps to winning I've outlined here. The Hoyt Foundation is a prime example of having a deep-seated purpose for competing, working with others, and giving back to the endeavor they loved.

My Story: Justification

Once in every life

There comes a time

We walk out all alone

And into the light

The moment won't last but then,

We remember it again

When we close our eyes

Andrea Bocelli *"Because We Believe"*

No Excuses, but?

Please understand the following is not an excuse. As an athlete, I know not to make excuses, so please consider the following an honest analysis with a twist. First, a legitimate reason for underperformance is my pace has slipped over the years. The truth is Father Time is winning the battle, as it did in my career. Of course, that is no reason to quit running; it's about coming to terms with the reality.

Here goes with my gripe.

I may be a little envious of the top marathoners, but it is no surprise they run in unbelievable finish times. They do not have to deal with the hindrances we, the grinders,

216

have. The leaders run the actual distance of 26.2 miles, and that's it. They have no one in front blocking their straight-line path. The top runners get to chase the TV vehicle, and that's it. The average Joe's (me) and Joanna's feel we are pushing it while weaving through rush hour traffic.

Many factors come into play to deter us from breaking records. The first of those is the amount of energy we spend getting to the race and the hours of waiting to begin it. And, if it is even possible, we must save a little strength for the trudge home afterward. At the end of most of my marathons, my distance application reads upwards of 30 miles on the day. Added to the total mileage are the extras of getting to and from the venue. That distance has one in the Ultrarunner category, so take that, world-class runners — 26.2 is nothing!

As hinted, a "bummer" is no straight line exists. The "average" must dart left and right, along with slowing to avoid collisions or getting tangled feet. Because of congestion, in one marathon, my family watched at miles 3 and 4 and never saw me go by, and it wasn't because I was going too fast!

Equally detrimental to running world-class times, runners like me have integrity. We have fans and relatives to see. We do not mind taking a ninety-degree turn to shake hands with supporters and stop to chat for a few minutes. We display our appreciation for their coming. The world-class runners do not perform such feats of courtesy. We, mortals, believe in those acts of friendship and are willing to sacrifice a couple of minutes of our time. Of course, we do not stop for the physical rest, but merely to offer thanks for the support. That's my story.

Also, the leaders do not stop and go to the bathroom four or five times as I do. I would like to see them out on the course for five hours and see how they enjoy waiting minutes to get a lovely stall.

Proof of Truth be Told

OK, that was with tongue in cheek. But some truth is in it. My latest marathon was the Marine Corps virtual marathon. Don't let the virtual word fool you. Twenty-six point two miles is the same, no matter the added description. A marathon is a marathon!

The cool part of a virtual run is the sense of being a professional Marathoner. I didn't have to deal with the mentioned hassles of getting to and from it. Usually, on race day, I wake hours before and begin the long haul of getting to the starting area. Then begins the long wait in the starting corral before shoving off. For the New York marathon, I had to catch a ride at 5 AM to get to the starting area, only to wait four hours before taking off. I felt exhausted way before running 26.2 miles. No excuses, I know, but really?

With the recent virtual race, I may have had a hundred steps to begin and headed out the door at the time of my choosing. There was no waiting area or other runners to play "footsie" with on the course. Even better, I began the virtual race in the lead, and not one runner passed me. See, I was comparable to the world elite marathon runners. Upon finishing, I felt I could have kept going a

218

few more miles. Beautiful, and I know I never had a similar sensation in my marathon past. It proves the extra work we hustlers have is a significant disadvantage and the Bigshot runners have it made. Once again, that's my stick-to-it story.

Unfortunately, I had the same finish time, and Father Time won again. Did I mention the strong winds I dealt with out there? Never mind.

It's on to marathon number 15. I hope it will be easier after having done it many times before. Unfortunately, another lesson from the baseball career is more work is necessary as you age, not less. So, the usual questions begin again, "Will I have what it takes?" And then the yearly one from my family, "Maybe it's time to drop to the half marathon?" My answer to the first is, "Who knows? I hope to, I plan to, but a long road lay ahead. To the second, with an annoyed expression, "No way, I'm not a half-type guy."

Home Again

Did you ever know that you're my hero?

And everything I would like to be

I can fly higher than an eagle

For you are the wind beneath my wings…

Thank you, thank you

Thank God for you, the wind beneath my wings

Bette Midler *"Wind Beneath My Wings"*

Summary

If you remember anything from the many steps provided, these are the things never to forget:

- Realizing dreams is not a given to anyone; you must earn them.

- Trying makes every attempt worthwhile. It's inaction that hurts. It's time to quit thinking and start doing!

- "Extraordinary" goes into making robust goals come true.

- Whether you attain or not, enjoy, rejoice, and move on; there are always other hills to climb.

- A hero is within everyone's grasp; it's a mindset you control.

I also said in the beginning running is a metaphor for life. However, one significant difference exists. The miles seem to last forever the further you go in a marathon. In life, the years pass by faster. Both are a race against time. **It's how you use your time that makes the difference.** I recall the movie *Groundhog Day*. In it, Bill Murray gets to repeat the same day until he gets it right. It' takes a while. That's what's great about sports — each day, game, and run allows us the opportunity to make it better than the previous ones. But, primarily, running mimics life – both provide the chance to fine-tune one's actions daily. It takes time to do it right, overcome disappointments, and deliver victories, but we shouldn't want it any other way.

Finally, I give thanks for the strength to run the race with perseverance, health, and help. **I know I have accomplished nothing in my life without support and sacrifice from others.** I had unbelievable backing growing up. The love mom, dad, and sisters gave helped my dreams come true. Now, inspiration comes from my wife, kids, and grandkids. Everything I do is for them, and any success I have is theirs and because of them. My writing has been a way of saying, "Thank you." to them, to whom I dedicate this song.

After all my strength is gone

In you, I can be strong

I look to you I look to you, oh yeah

And when melodies are gone

In you, I hear a song

I look to you

Whitney Houston – I Look to You

For one final pep talk, **"Don't stop when you are tired, only when done."**

About the Author

Former Major League Ballplayer Jack Perconte combines his Major League Baseball playing and marathon running experience here in his fourth book. He is the author of *Creating a Season to Remember, Raising an Athlete*, and *The Making of a Hitter*.